OCS EIS/EA
MMS 2008-026

Programmatic Environmental Assessment for Grid 9

I0411832

Site-Specific Evaluation of Energy Resource Technology, Inc.'s Supplemental Development Operations Coordination Document, S-7156

Phoenix Project
Green Canyon Blocks 236 and 237

Author

Minerals Management Service
Gulf of Mexico OCS Region

U.S. Department of the Interior
Minerals Management Service
Gulf of Mexico OCS Region

New Orleans
May 2008

FINDING OF NO SIGNIFICANT IMPACT

Energy Resource Technology, Inc.'s (ERT) Supplemental Development Operations Coordination Document (DOCD) to drill, complete, and produce from six new wells—Wells A and B in Green Canyon Block 236 (OCS-G 15562) and Wells A, B, C, and D in Green Canyon Block 237 (OCS-G 15563)—has been reviewed. Also proposed in their Supplemental DOCD, ERT plans to install a subsea manifold, clear the location of debris, and install a floating production unit in Green Canyon Block 237.

Our programmatic environmental assessment (PEA) on this proposed action (S-7156) is complete and results in a Finding of No Significant Impact. Based on this PEA, we have concluded that the proposed action will not significantly affect the quality of the human environment (40 CFR 1508.27). Preparation of an environmental impact statement is not required. The following mitigation is necessary to ensure environmental protection, consistent environmental policy, and safety as required by the National Environmental Policy Act, as amended, or is a recommended measure needed for compliance with 40 CFR 1500.2(f) regarding the requirement for Federal agencies to avoid or minimize any possible adverse effects of their action upon the quality of the human environment.

Mitigation 8.03 (Advisory)—H_2S Absent

The area in which the proposed drilling operations are to be conducted is hereby classified as "H_2S absent," in accordance with 30 CFR 250.417(c). The location and depths of the planned wells are not expected to encounter an H_2S hazard. An H_2S Contingency Plan is not required to be submitted and approved by the MMS prior to ERT conducting the proposed activities. (8.03)

Gary Goeke,
Supervisor, NEPA/CZM Coordination Unit
Leasing and Environment
Gulf of Mexico OCS Region

May 27, 08
Date

Dennis Chew
Chief, Environmental Assessment Section
Leasing and Environment
Gulf of Mexico OCS Region

5/27/08
Date

Joseph A. Christopher
Regional Supervisor
Leasing and Environment
Gulf of Mexico OCS Region

5/27/08
Date

TABLE OF CONTENTS

FIGURES

TABLES

ABBREVIATIONS AND ACRONYMS

ac	acre
bbl	barrel
BOD	biochemical oxygen demand
BSL	below sea level
CFR	Code of Federal Regulations
CO	carbon monoxide
CPA	Central Planning Area
CZM	Coastal Zone Management
DOCD	Development Operations Coordination Document
DOI	Department of the Interior
DP	dynamically positioned
DTS	disconnectable transfer system
E&P	exploration and production
EFH	essential fish habitat
EIA	economic impact area
EIS	environmental impact statement
EPA	Eastern Planning Area
ERT	Energy Resource Technology, Inc.
ESA	Endangered Species Act
FAA	Federal Aviation Administration
FEL	from the east block line
FPU	floating production unit
FNL	from the north block line
FSL	from the south block line
ft	feet
FWL	from the west block line
gal	gallon
GC	Green Canyon
GMFMC	Gulf of Mexico Fishery Management Council
GOM	Gulf of Mexico
GS	Geological Survey
ha	hectares
H_2S	hydrogen sulfide
km	kilometer
L	liter
LA Hwy 1	Louisiana Highway 1
LMA	Labor Market Area
m	meter
MARPOL	International Convention for the Prevention of Pollution from Ships
mi	mile
MMS	Minerals Management Service
MODU	mobile offshore drilling unit
MWA	Military Warning Area
NAAQS	National Ambient Air Quality Standards
NEPA	National Environmental Policy Act
NERBC	New England River Basins Commission
NMFS	National Marine Fisheries Service
NO_x	nitrogen oxides
NO_2	nitrogen dioxide
NOAA	National Oceanic and Atmospheric Administration
NPDES	National Pollutant Discharge and Elimination System
NRC	National Research Council
NTL	Notice to Lessees and Operators

OCS	Outer Continental Shelf
OCSLA	Outer Continental Shelf Lands Act
PAH	polynuclear aromatic hydrocarbon
PCB	polychlorinated biphenyl
PEA	Programmatic Environmental Assessment
PM	particulate matter
ppt	parts per thousand
PSD	Prevention of Significant Deterioration
QCDC	Quick Connect Disconnect Connector
ROV	remotely operated vehicle
SBF	synthetic-based fluid
SOV	spill occurrence variable
SO_x	sulphur oxides
SWAMP	Sperm Whale Acoustic Monitoring Program
SWSS	Sperm Whale Seismic Study
TLP	tension-leg platform
TV	transport variable
U.S.	United States
USDOC	U.S. Department of Commerce
USDOI	U.S. Department of the Interior
USDOT	U.S. Department of Transportation
USEPA	U.S. Environmental Protection Agency
USCG	U.S. Coast Guard
VOC	volatile organic compounds
WBF	water-based fluid
WPA	Western Planning Area
yr	year

INTRODUCTION

The Minerals Management Service (MMS) developed a comprehensive strategy for postlease National Environmental Policy Act (NEPA) compliance for development and production projects in deepwater areas (water depths greater than 400 meters (m) (1,312 feet (ft)) in the Central Planning Area (CPA) and Western Planning Area (WPA) of the Gulf of Mexico (GOM). The strategy led to the development of a biologically-based grid system to ensure broad and systematic analysis of the GOM's deepwater region, which is explained on MMS's website at http://www.mms.gov. This strategy divides the deepwater Gulf into 18 areas or "grids" of biological similarity, which generally correlate to water depth.

The area for this programmatic environmental assessment (PEA) is Grid 9 in the CPA. Grid 9 is a portion of the Outer Continental Shelf (OCS) in water depths between 400 and 1,000 m (1,312 and 3,280 ft). **Figure 1** shows the relationship of Grid 9 to the Gulf's coastline and the other 17 grids. This PEA characterizes the environment of Grid 9 and examines the potential impacts that may result from the site-specific activities proposed by Energy Resource Technology, Inc. (ERT) in its Supplemental Development Operations Coordination Documents (DOCD) (Plan Number S-7156) for their proposed Phoenix Project. ERT proposes to use a floating production unit (FPU) to receive and export produced oil and gas. The MMS has determined that the Phoenix Project is a suitable project on which to base this PEA since it proposes to install surface facilities in waterdepths >400 m (1,312 ft) and is centrally located in and representative of Grid 9.

The PEA is designed to be comprehensive in terms of (1) characterizing the physical, biological, and socioeconomic resources within the grid, (2) describing the impact-producing factors from this proposed development project, (3) describing the potential impacts from this specific proposal that are representative of the grid, and (4) considering the cumulative impacts from OCS development activity within Grid 9. **Figure 2** shows the location of the proposed Phoenix Project in Green Canyon Blocks 236 and 237 (OCS-G 15562 and 15563, respectively) in relationship to the 221 OCS blocks that comprise Grid 9.

The Grid 9 PEA serves as a reference document for the tiering (40 CFR 1502.20) concept detailed in NEPA's implementing regulations and allows subsequent environmental analyses for individual plans proposed within the grid to focus on specific issues and effects within Grid 9. This PEA tiers primarily from *Gulf of Mexico OCS Oil and Gas Lease Sales: 2007-2012; Western Planning Area Sales 204, 207, 210, 215, and 218; Central Planning Area Sales 205, 206, 208, 213, 216, and 222; Final Environmental Impact Statement; Volumes I and II* (Multisale EIS) (USDOI, MMS, 2007). Relevant information from the Multisale EIS is hereby incorporated by reference into this PEA.

Current Status of Grid 9

Figure 1 shows the relationship of Grid 9 to the Gulf's coastline and the other 17 grids that have been defined in MMS's comprehensive strategy for postlease NEPA compliance in deepwater areas of the GOM. The nearest land to Grid 9 is in Isle Denieres in Terrebonne Parish, Louisiana, approximately 70 miles (mi) (113 kilometers (km)) to the north (**Figure 1**). **Figure 2** shows the OCS protraction areas and blocks within Grid 9 and the location of the Phoenix Project in Green Canyon Blocks 236 and 237.

1

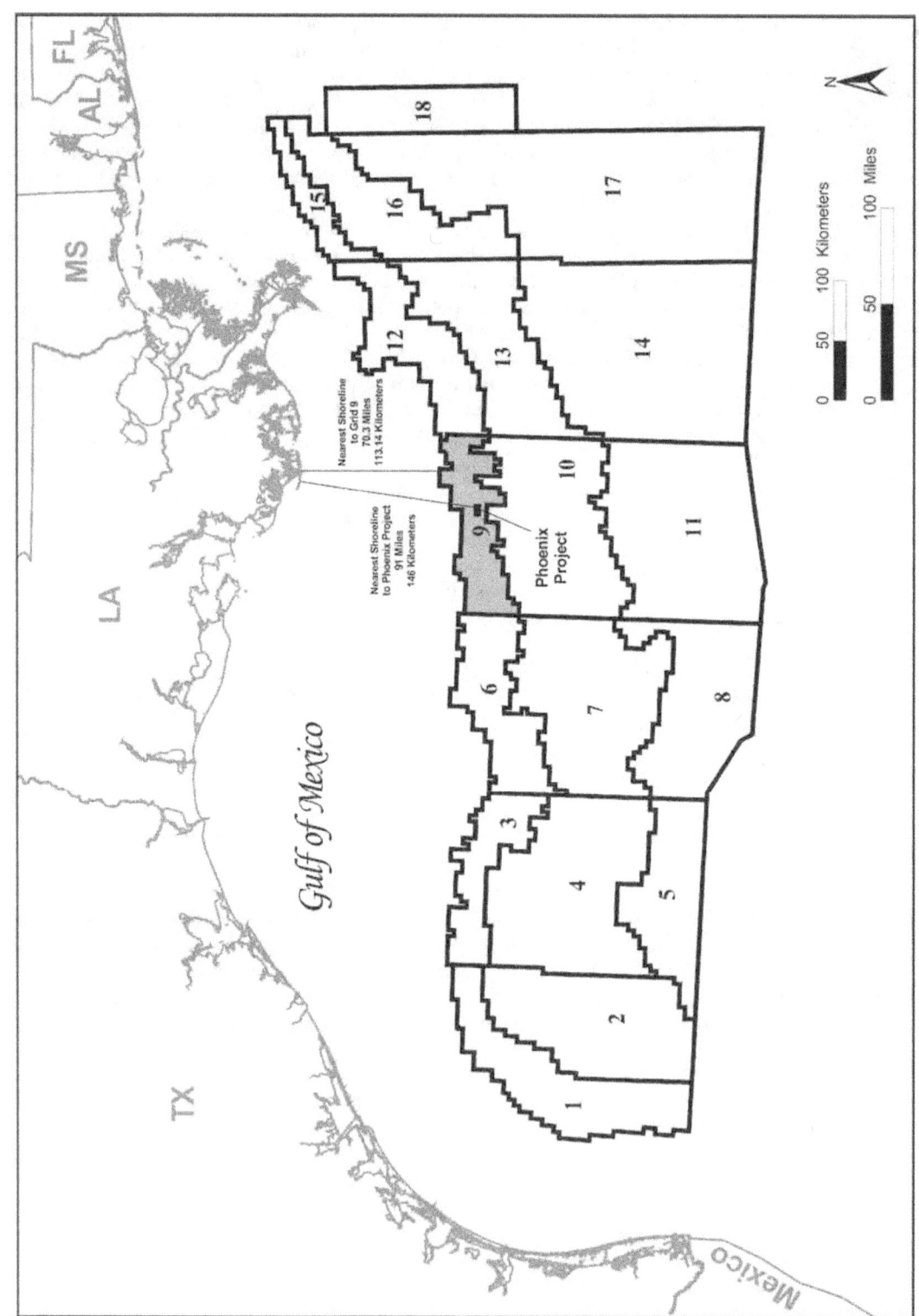

Figure 1. Relationship of Grid 9 to the Gulf Coastline and to Other Grids Defined in MMS's Comprehensive Deepwater Development Strategy.

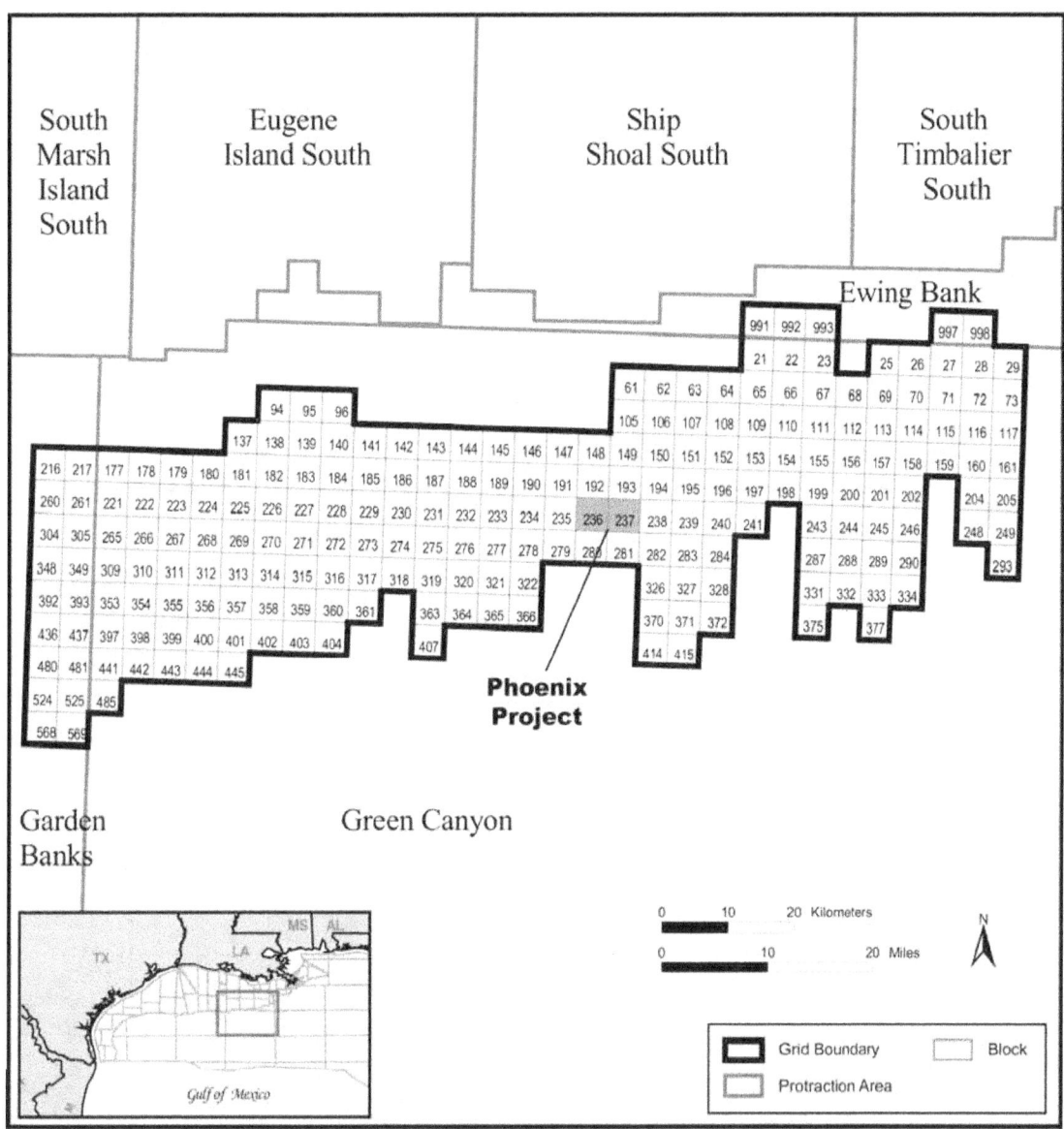

Figure 2. Areas and Blocks in Grid 9 with the Location of the Proposed Phoenix Project.

Table 1 summarizes the statistics for the OCS areas of Green Canyon, Ewing Bank, and Garden Banks, which constitute Grid 9. Green Canyon constitutes about 89 percent of the total number of blocks in Grid 9 and about 90 percent of the total number of leases. Ewing Bank constitutes 3 percent of the total number of blocks in Grid 9 and about 3 percent of the total leases; Garden Banks contains the remaining 8 percent of the total number of blocks in Grid 9 and 7 percent of the total leases. About 78 percent of all blocks in the grid are leased. **Figure 3** shows the bathymetry of Grid 9. **Figure 4** shows the location of the Military Warning Areas (MWA's) relative to Grid 9. About 30 percent of Grid 9 (70 whole and partial blocks) lies within portions of three MWA's. Approximately 1 percent (approximately 3 whole and partial blocks) of Grid 9 lies in MWA W-147AB, approximately 6.5 percent (approximately 15 whole and partial blocks) lies in MWA W-59A, and approximately 23 percent (approximately 51 whole and partial blocks) lies within MWA W-92. Green Canyon Blocks 236 and 237 lie outside the three MWA's. Although Green Canyon Blocks 236 and 237 lie outside the above-mentioned MWA's, the lessee is required to enter into an agreement with the commander of the individual headquarters, listed in **Table 2**, upon utilizing an individual designated warning area prior to commencing an operation on its behalf, via a boat, ship, or a aircraft traffic into one of the MWA's. Such an agreement will provide for the positive control of boats, ships, and aircraft operating into the warning areas at all times.

Table 1

Protraction Areas, Blocks, and Leases in Grid 9

Protraction Area	No. of Grid Blocks	No. of Grid Blocks Leased	Percentage of Grid Blocks Leased
Green Canyon	197	155	77
Ewing Bank	6	5	83
Garden Banks	18	12	67
Grid Totals	221	172	78

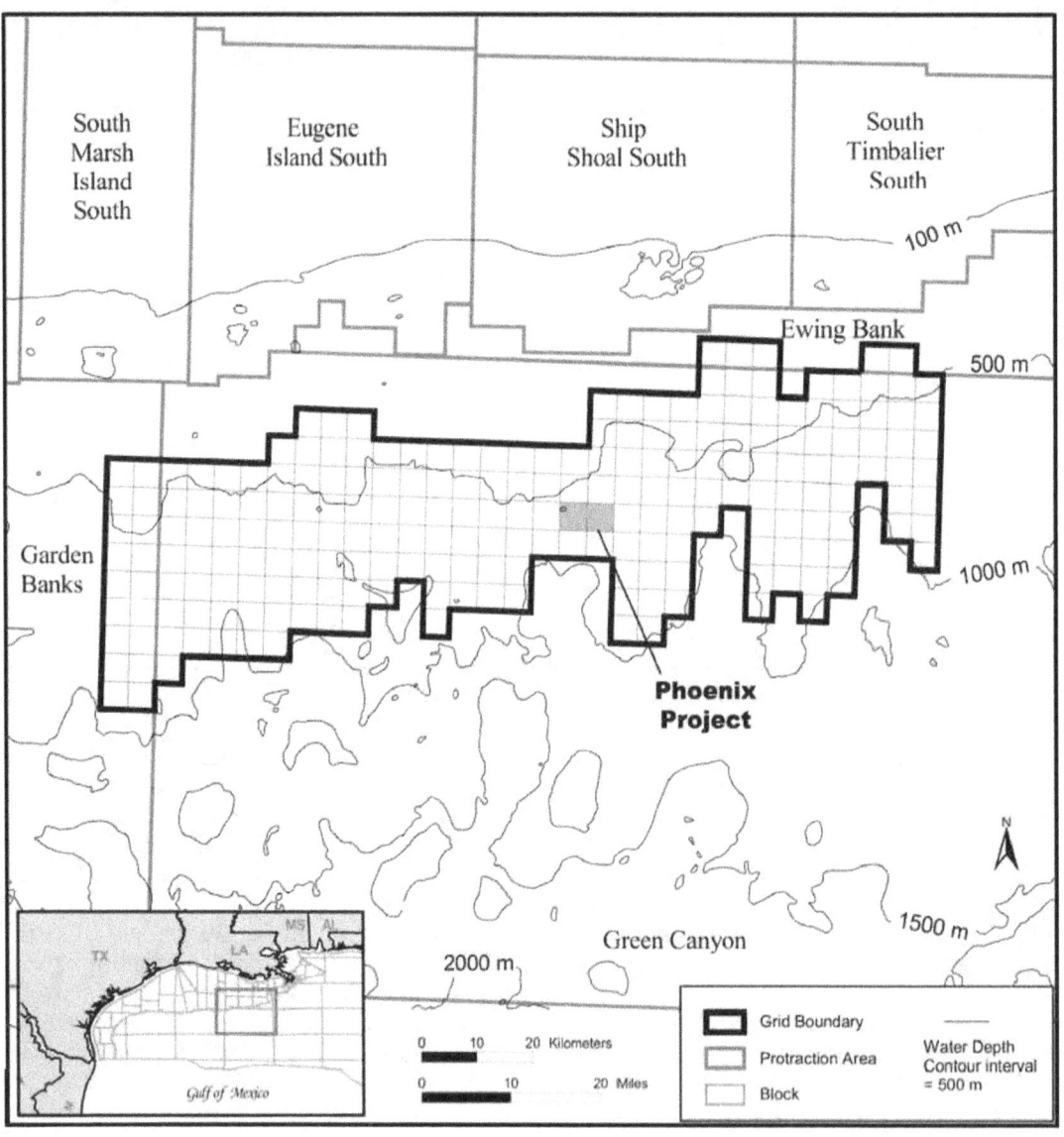

Figure 3. Bathymetric Map of Grid 9.

4

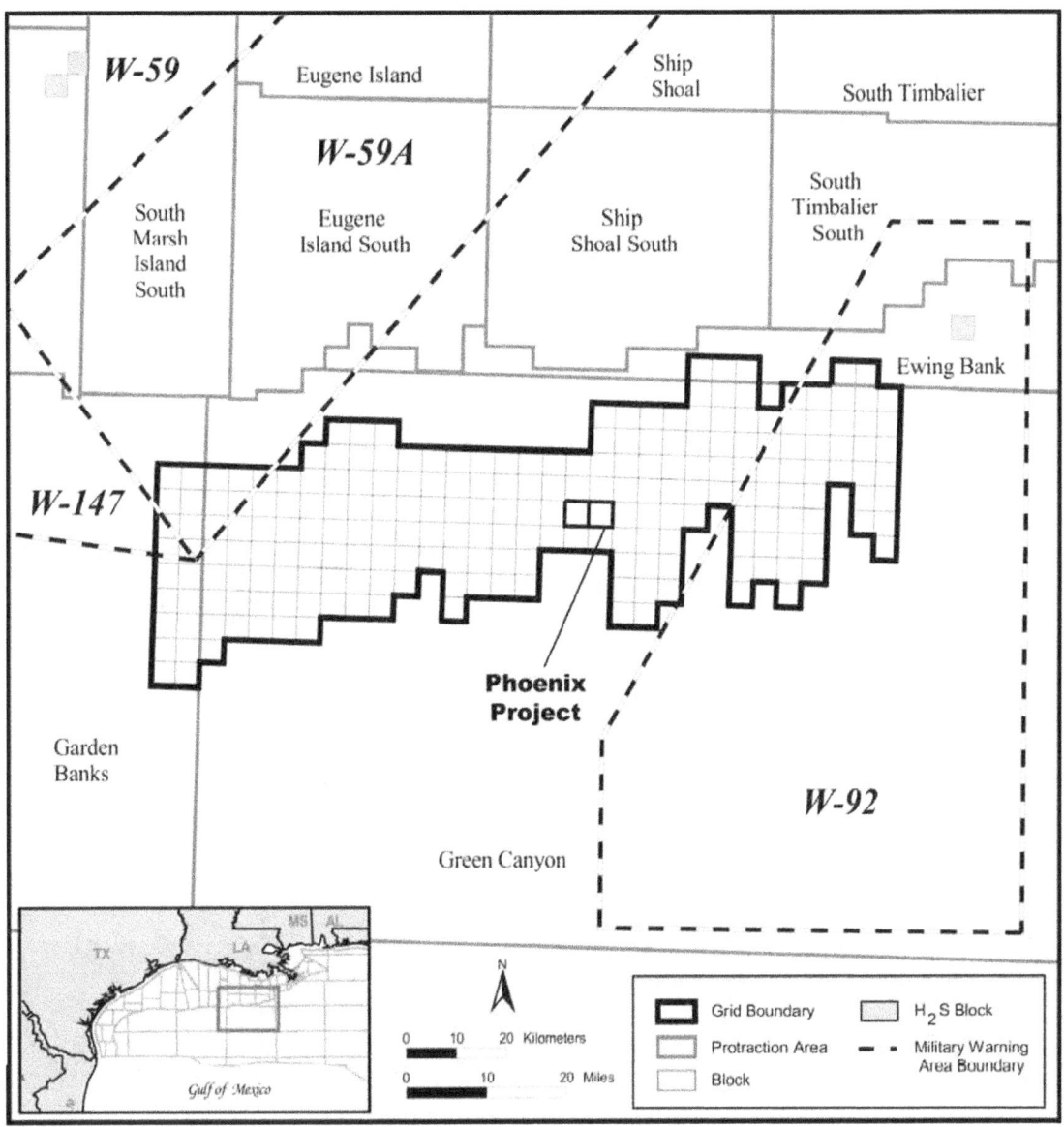

Figure 4. Military Warning Areas Proximal to Grid 9.

Table 2

Grid 9 Military Warning Areas and Headquarters Addresses

Military Warning Area	Command Headquarters
W-59	Naval Air Station JRB 159 Fighter Wing 400 Russell Avenue, Box 27 Building 285 New Orleans, Louisiana 70143-0027 Telephone: (504) 391-8696
W-92	Naval Air Station Air Operations Department Air traffic Division/Code 52 400 Russell Avenue, Building 1 New Orleans, Louisiana 70143-0027 Telephone: (504) 678-3101
W-147	147 OG/DOV 14657 Sneider Street Houston, Texas 77034-5586 Telephone: (281) 929-2142

Operators and/or leaseholders in Grid 9 are shown in **Table 3**. At present, there are 33 operators and/or leaseholders in Grid 9. These operators include major international oil and gas operators as well as independent companies. This listing reflects MMS's databases at the time this PEA was written. Interest by leasehold may vary over time.

Table 3

Owners and/or Leasholders in Grid 9

Anadarko E&P Company LP	LLOG Exploration Offshore, Inc.
BHP Billiton Petroleum (GOM) Inc.	Marathon Oil Company
BP Exploration & Production Inc.	Mariner Energy, Inc.
Capco Offshore, Inc.	Marubeni Oil & Gas (USA) Inc.
Chevron U.S.A. Inc.	Murphy Exploration & Production Company—USA
Cobalt International Energy, L.P.	Nexen Petroleum Offshore U.S.A. Inc.
ConocoPhillips Company	Nexen Petroleum U.S.A. Inc.
Davis Offshore, L.P.	Noble Energy, Inc.
Deep Gulf Energy LP	Plains Exploration & Production Company
Devon Energy Production Company, L.P.	Remington Oil and Gas Corporation
Energy Resource Technology, Inc.	Repsol E&P USA Inc.
Energy XXI GOM, LLC	Royal Production Company, Inc
Eni US Operating Co. Inc.	Shell Offshore Inc.
Exxon Mobil Corporation	Stone Energy Corporation
Hess Corporation	W&T Offshore, Inc.
Hydro Gulf of Mexico, L.L.C.	Walter O & G Corporation
Kerr-McGee Oil & Gas Corporation	

The type of lease and the status of plans that have been submitted in Grid 9 are shown in **Figure 5**. In Grid 9, there were 94 exploration plans and 52 DOCD's approved by MMS. Nineteen blocks have been designated by their operators as unit developments.

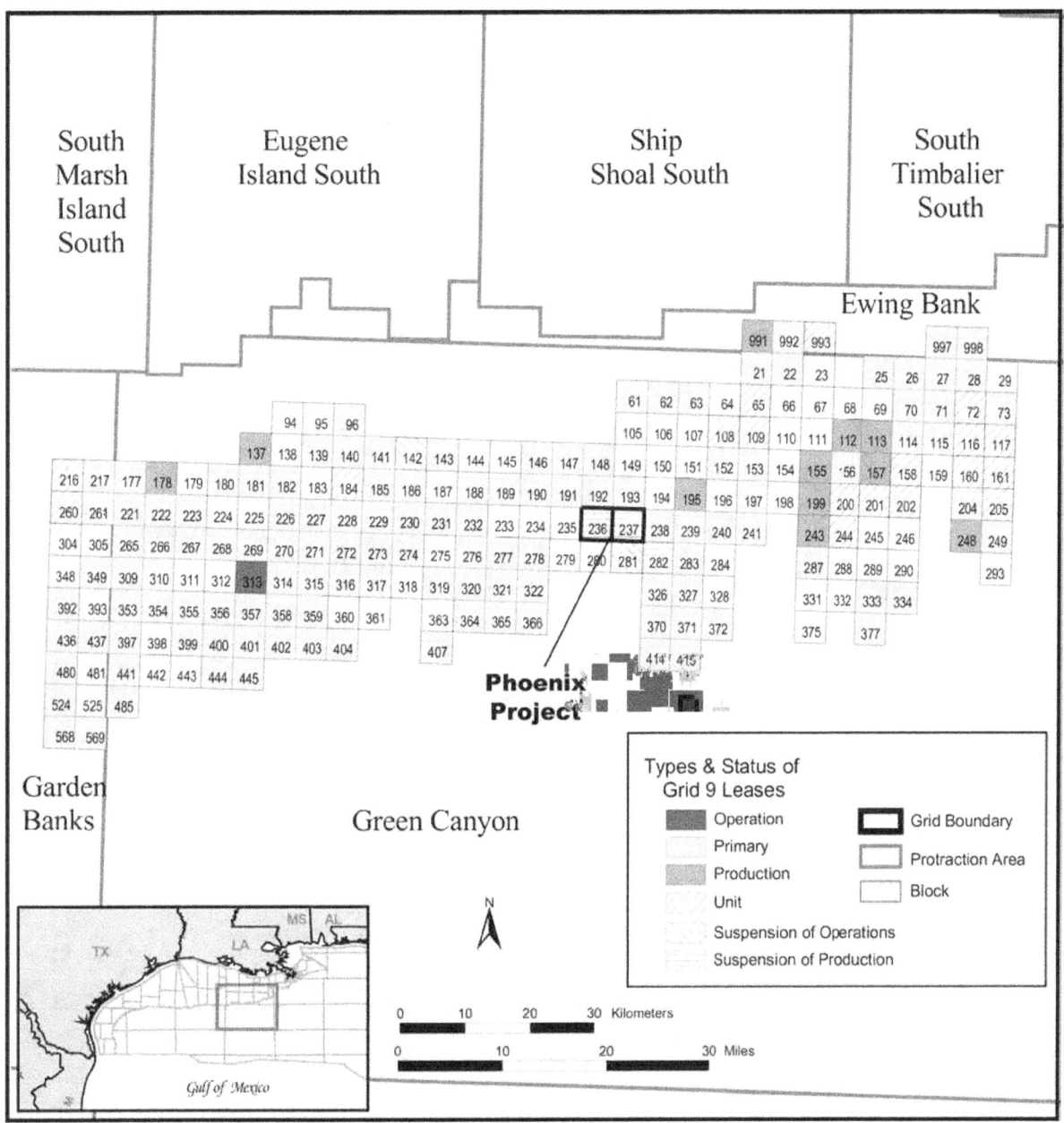

Figure 5. Active Lease Status and Plans Submitted in Grid 9.

ERT has chosen Port Fourchon, Louisiana, as its onshore base to support its offshore operations for the Phoenix Project. This base is widely used by industry. There are numerous onshore support bases that are available along the Gulf Coast and that could serve as logistical infrastructure for Grid 9. **Figure 6** shows the distances from the Phoenix Project in Green Canyon Blocks 236 and 237 to ERT's chosen shore base.

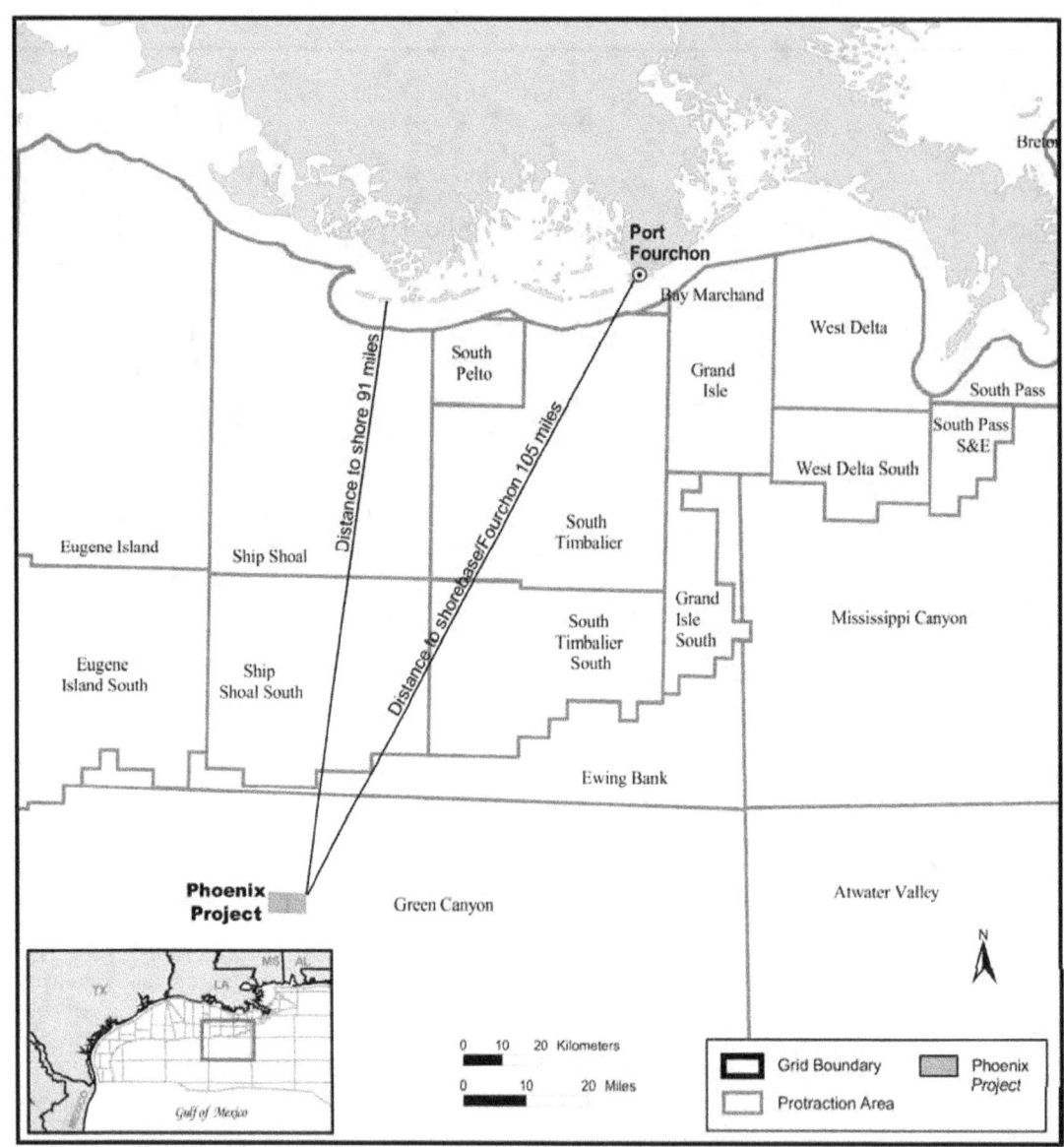

Figure 6. Distances from the Phoenix Project in Green Canyon Blocks 236 and 237 to the
Primary Shore Bases in Port Fourchon, Louisiana, and the Closest Shoreline.

1. PROPOSED ACTION

1.1. PURPOSE OF THE PROPOSED ACTION

The purpose of the proposed action outlined by ERT in their DOCD is to drill, complete, and produce the hydrocarbon resources in Green Canyon Blocks 236 and 237. Exploration, discovery, and production of hydrocarbon resources would help satisfy the Nation's need for energy. Under the Outer Continental Shelf Lands Act (OCSLA), as amended, the Department of the Interior (DOI) is required to manage the orderly leasing, exploration, development, and production of oil and gas resources on the Federal OCS. The Secretary of the Interior oversees the OCS oil and gas program and MMS is the agency charged with this oversight. The Secretary is required to balance orderly resource development with protection of the human, marine, and coastal environments while ensuring that the U.S. public receives an equitable return for resources discovered and produced on public lands.

1.2. NEED FOR THE PROPOSED ACTION

As the designated operator of Green Canyon Blocks 236 and 237, ERT filed a DOCD with MMS consistent with its obligation to file such a plan before exploration activity commences. Listed below are some of the reasons that ERT has submitted this proposal to MMS:

- leaseholders have a legal right to pursue exploration for and development and production of hydrocarbon resources;

- leaseholders are obligated via lease terms to diligently develop the resources; and

- a lease term is limited to 10 years and failure to identify and develop resources could lead to loss of the sunk costs to acquire the lease, as well as yearly rentals to maintain access to the lease.

1.3. DESCRIPTION OF THE PROPOSED ACTION

1.3.1. Proposed Action

Energy Resource Technology, Inc. submitted a Supplemental DOCD to MMS on November 15, 2007. ERT subsequently provided additional information regarding the plan that allowed MMS to determine it to be complete. In its DOCD, ERT proposes to drill and complete two new wells in Green Canyon Block 236 (OCS-G 15562) and four new wells in Green Canyon Block 237 (OCS-G 15563), install a subsea manifold, clear the location and install an FPU in Green Canyon Block 237, and commence production from Green Canyon Blocks 236 and 237 (ERT, 2007).

Measured liquid hydrocarbons from Green Canyon Blocks 236 and 237 would be brought to the FPU in Green Canyon Block 237, the Helix Producer 1 (HP1) platform, where it would be transported via Enterprise Field Services' 12-inch pipeline (Segment No. 12780) that connects to Shell Offshore Inc.'s Green Canyon Block 19 A platform for ultimate delivery to shore via Operations System No. 29.5 and/or Operations System No. 36.5. The Measured gas will depart the Green Canyon Block 237 HP1 platform via ANR Central Gulf Gathering Company, Inc.'s 20-inch pipeline (Segment No. 12749) that connects to Eugene Island Area Block 371 A platform for ultimate delivery to shore via Operations System No. 24.0.

ERT will use a typical dynamically positioned (DP) semisubmersible drilling rig for the drilling and completion operations of the proposed wells.

Associated Action and Activities

Effective August 23, 2006, ERT was designated operator of Leases OCS-G 15562, 15563, 16727, and 26302 for Green Canyon Blocks 236, 237, 282, and 238, respectively. ERT previously submitted to MMS application(s) to install 19 lease-term pipelines. ERT plans to reestablish production from the former Typhoon and Boris Fields. The Typhoon tension-leg platform (TLP), flowlines, and umbilicals were destroyed and severed by Hurricane Rita in September 2005 and will be replaced with similar components to reconnect the wells to a subsea manifold which would be connected to the DP floating production unit (Helix Producer 1). Thirteen of the lease-term pipelines would be installed initially to produce the existing five wells in Green Canyon Blocks 237 and 282 (Green Canyon Block 237, Wells #001, #003, and #004 (Typhoon Field); Green Canyon Block 282, Wells #001 and #002 (Boris Field)) and a sixth well adjacent to the Boris Field, Green Canyon 238, Well #001 (Little Burn), which is not part of this proposed action. Those 13 pipelines would later be connected, and production would commence from the previously-mentioned existing five wells in Green Canyon Blocks 237 and 282 (ERT, 2007). This is part of ERT's intention to reestablish production from five of the six wells that were being produced through the Typhoon TLP.

1.3.2. Background

Green Canyon Blocks 236 and 237 are located approximately 91 mi (146 km) southward from the nearest shoreline in Louisiana (i.e., Isle Dernieres, Terrebonne Parish) and approximately 105 mi (169 km) from the supply base at Port Fourchon in Lafourche Parish, Louisiana (**Figure 6**).

Figure 1 shows the location of Green Canyon Blocks 236 and 237 and the distance to the nearest shoreline from those blocks and the nearest shoreline from Grid 9. **Table 1-1** shows the location data for the FPU, the six proposed wells, and the disconnectable transfer system (DTS) in ERT's DOCD.

Table 1-1

Surface Locations of the Proposed Wells, Floating Production Unit, Disconnectable Transfer System, and Pipeline End Manifold

Location of Activity	Well Surface Location	Water Depth
Install Helix Producer 1 in GC 237	6,908' FNL; 2,885' FWL X=2,252,169.59' ; Y=10,067,331.95'	2,085'
Drill and complete GC 236 Well A	4,109' FNL; 4,275' FEL X=2,245,005' ; Y=10,070,131'	1,790'
Drill and complete GC 237 Well A	7,191' FNL; 4,344' FWL X=2,253,624' ; Y=10,067,049'	2,050'
Drill and complete GC 236 Well B	1,674' FNL; 5,617' FWL X=2,239,057' ; Y=10,072,566'	1,630'
Drill and complete GC 237 Well B	1,991' FSL; 2,442' FWL X=2,251,722' ; Y=10,060,391'	2,405'
Drill and complete GC 237 Well C	5,112' FSL; 3,293' FWL X=2,252,573' ; Y=10,063,512'	2,235'
Drill and complete GC 237 Well D	3,978' FSL; 2,633' FEL X=2,262,487' ; Y=10,062,378'	2,335'
Install Pipeline End Manifold in GC 237	3,300' FSL; 6,500' FWL X=2,265,668.27' ; Y=10,061,708.83'	2,360'
Install DTS in GC 237	6,908.05' FNL; 2,885.59' FWL X=2,252,165.59' ; Y=10,067,331.95'	2,085'

FEL = from the east block line, FNL = from the north block line, FSL = from the south block line, FWL = from the west block line, GC = Green Canyon.

1.3.3. Schedule of Activities

The drilling, completion, and installation program for the six wells and FPU proposed in the DOCD is scheduled to begin on October 1, 2008, with an estimated completion date of May 2013. The planned duration of drilling for the proposed action, i.e., to drill, complete, and produce the six new wells, is approximately 60 days (approximately 8 weeks) for each new well. Installation a lease-term pipeline(s) segment(s) to commence production from each new well should take from 10 to 15 days. ERT reports that it will produce from the six new wells and will restore production and produce from the five existing wells for a duration of five years. ERT provided the schedule shown in **Table 1-2**.

Table 1-2

Schedule for Pipelaying, Drilling, Completion, and Production from Green Canyon Blocks 236 and 237

Activity	Estimated Start Date	Estimated End Date	Days Duration
Install 13 lease-term pipelines in GC 236 and 237	02/01/08	03/21/08	50 days
Hookup and commence production from existing wells in GC 237 and 282	09/01/08	09/01/13	5 years
Drill and complete GC 237, Well A	10/01/08	11/29/08	60 days
Drill and complete GC 237, Well B	12/02/08	01/30/09	60 days
Install 2 lease-term pipelines	06/01/09	06/15/09	15 days
Hookup and produce GC 237, Wells A and B	07/01/09	07/01/14	5 years
Drill and complete GC 236, Well A	03/01/10	04/29/10	60 days
Install 1 lease-term pipeline	05/01/10	05/10/10	10 days
Hookup and produce GC 236, Well A	05/20/10	05/20/15	5 years
Drill and complete GC 236, Well B	03/01/11	04/29/11	60 days
Install 1 lease-term pipeline	05/01/11	05/10/11	10 days
Hookup and produce GC 236, Well B	05/20/11	05/20/16	5 years
Drill and complete GC 237, Well C	03/01/12	04/29/12	60 days
Install 1 lease-term pipeline	05/01/12	05/10/12	10 days
Hookup and produce GC 237, Well C	05/20/12	05/20/17	5 years
Drill and complete GC 237, Well D	03/01/13	04/29/13	60 days
Install 1 lease-term pipeline	05/01/13	05/10/13	10 days
Hookup and produce GC 237, Well D	05/20/13	05/20/18	5 years

GC = Green Canyon.

1.3.4. Equipment and Drilling System

ERT proposes to use a DP semisubmersible to drill the six new wells in Green Canyon Blocks 236 and 237. The specifications of the rig chosen by ERT for the proposed action would be made a part of the Application for Permit to Drill.

1.3.5. Support Facilities

Supply and crewboats and aircraft (helicopter) facilities to support the proposed action are located in Port Fourchon in Lafourche Parish, Louisiana, 105 mi (169 km) north-northeast of the project location (Figure 6). Existing onshore base facilities located in Port Fourchon, Louisiana, will be used as the debarkation point for equipment, supplies, and crews. ERT does not expect any shore base construction or expansion in association with this proposed operation.

1.3.6. Transportation Operations

Personal vehicles would be the main means of transportation to carry rig personnel from permanent or temporary residences to the Port Fourchon shore base. Personnel will then be transported to the drilling rig by the crewboat or helicopter. Supply boats will transport bulk supplies. The most practical, direct route permitted by the weather and traffic conditions would be used. The transportation route by service vessel is approximately 105 mi (169 km) to Green Canyon Blocks 236 and 237. The type of support vessels and travel frequency per week during drilling and completion operations are shown in **Table 1-3**.

Table 1-3

Support Vessel and Frequency

Support Vessel	Trips/Week	Maximum Number in Area at Any Time
Crewboats–personnel and supplies	2	1
Supply boats–bulk supplies and casing	2	1
Helicopter–personnel and small supplies	3	1

1.3.7. New and Unusual Technology

ERT proposes to use a disconnectable transfer system (DTS) for the proposed development of the Phoenix Field. The DTS allows disconnection from the flowlines, pipelines, and umbilicals. The riser system, which will be buoyed by six mooring lines, will enable the ship to disconnect and seek shelter from severe weather and during conditions when position cannot be maintained. The mooring lines do not provide any station-keeping service.

1.3.8. Impacts from Potential Geological Hazards

The MMS approved ERT's request to use 3D exploration data for the shallow hazards assessment for Wells A and B in Green Canyon Block 237 on July 10, 2007, and for Wells A and B in Green Canyon Block 236 and Wells C and D in Green Canyon Block 237 on September 21, 2007. The MMS has received adequate, remotely operated vehicle (ROV) survey coverage for Grid 9; therefore, ERT is not required to conduct ROV surveys for the proposed operations, except during pre-spudding and post-drilling operations.

Key seafloor hazards that may affect proposed activities include steep slopes, debris from Hurricane Rita in September 2005, faults, shallow water flow, and shallow gas. Slopes at the proposed wells and FPU sites are in a southward direction and range from 1.2° to 2.5°. Debris from the Typhoon TLP, its associated flowlines, and umbilicals would be cleared from the seafloor location of the six proposed wells and would not be closer than 845 ft (257 m) to any proposed well (Green Canyon Block 236, Well A). A fault scarp exists as close as 610 ft (186 m) to Green Canyon Block 236, Well A and 700 ft (213 m) northeast of Green Canyon Block 236, Well B. No high negative or high positive amplitude anomalies associated with fluid expulsion or mounded carbonates representing potential chemosynthetic communities were noted within a 1,500-ft (457-m) radius of the proposed well sites. One mound is found 1,554 ft (474 m) to the northwest of Green Canyon Block 236, Well B and should be avoided. Green Canyon Block 236 is not classified by MMS as a "shallow-water, up flow area," although Green Canyon Block 237 is. Shallow water flows occur when sands lie below a seal, which prevents dewatering and compaction, and in unconsolidated and overpressured sands. The pressure rises with overburden and presents a potential hazard for drilling. Shallow gas potential also exists in the Grid 9 area. A moderate to high amplitude anomaly was noted 4,488 ft (1,368 m) below sea-level (BSL) (Green Canyon Block 236, Well A). Setting the first casing string above the anomaly at this wellsite is recommended.

1.4. OFFSHORE DISCHARGES AND WASTE DISPOSAL

The discharge of wastes into offshore waters is regulated by the U.S. Environmental Protection Agency (USEPA) under the authority of the Clean Water Act. No wastes generated during oil and gas operations can be discharged overboard unless they meet the standards required within a National Pollution Discharge Elimination System (NPDES) permit. All of the waste types generated from the proposed exploration activities for the Phoenix Project will be either (1) discharged overboard in compliance with NPDES requirements or (2) transported to shore for disposal in permitted or licensed commercial facilities or for recycling. The wastes for overboard discharge are summarized in **Table 1-4**.

Table 1-4

Projected Ocean Discharges from the Phoenix Project

Type of Waste	Total Amount Discharged	Discharge Rate	Discharge Method
Spent Drilling Fluids	2,500/well	220 bbl/hour	Discharged at the surface.
Synthetic-based Fluids	NA	NA	Recycle and discharged at the surface.
Deck Drainage	0-365 bbl/yr (dependent upon rainfall)	1 bbl/day	Treated to remove oil and grease. Discharged overboard.
Produced Water	250,000 bbl/yr	1,000 bbl/day	Pipe to a well on lease, inject to downhole/Wemco discharge overboard.

Wastes generated during the development and production activities of the Phoenix Project consist of (1) drill fluids; (2) drill cuttings (water-based fluids (WBF); (3) deck drainage; (4) sanitary and domestic wastes; (5) uncontaminated seawater used for cooling, desalinization, and ballast; (6) excess cement, (7) well treatment, workover, or completion fluids; (8) bilge water; (9) chemically treated seawater or freshwater; (10) used oil; and (11) solid trash and debris. Well treatment, completion, and workover fluids would be collected in a separator. Aqueous fluids would be routed to the water treatment system for discharge. Nonaqueous fluids would be collected in drums or the slop tank of a supply vessel to be transported to shore for disposal.

Routine sanitary and domestic wastes necessarily arise from people working offshore on drilling rigs, production platforms, and support vessels. Estimates of the amounts of sanitary and domestic wastes discharged from associated service-vessel operations were not provided by ERT but are generally estimated to be 60 gallons (gal)/person/day (NERBC, 1976).

Deck drainage effluent is primarily rainwater containing residual oil and grease from equipment washwater and rainwater. Overboard discharge of deck drainage is governed by the NPDES permit requirement for no visible oil sheen. A maximum for deck drainage during daily operation is estimated by MMS to be 3,000 barrels (bbl) per month.

1.5. POTENTIAL IMPACT-PRODUCING FACTORS

Physical Disturbances to the Seafloor

Physical disturbance of the seafloor will occur during installation, operation, and decommissioning. Seafloor impacts will result from (1) pipeline installation; (2) the installation of subsea production equipment including well trees, manifolds, flowline sleds, etc.; (3) and the installation of flowlines and umbilicals. The FPU will be kept in place via a DP2 dynamic positioning system. The riser system will enable the ship to disconnect and seek shelter from severe weather and during conditions when position cannot be maintained. The risers are connected to a buoy that will sink approximately 45 m (148 ft) when disconnected. The buoy is moored via six anchor chains, each 3,000 ft (914 m) long, which serve to keep the buoy in place. The mooring lines do not provide any station-keeping service.

Subsea production equipment is assumed to include 1 FPU, 1 manifold, and 19 lease-term pipelines. The installation and eventual decommissioning of all subsea production equipment will directly disturb the seafloor.

The 19 lease-term pipelines will be installed by a DP pipelaying barge. Because a DP pipelaying barge will be used for the lease-term pipelines, there will be no anchoring along the pipeline route. Since the water depth is greater than 200 ft (61 m) for the entire route, burial is not required. Therefore, the area affected by pipelaying is limited to the seafloor immediately beneath the pipe.

Effluent Discharges

Effluent discharges will include discharges from vessels involved in facility installation, discharges during drilling and completion operations, and discharges from support vessels. Estimated waste discharges are quantified in **Chapter 1.4**.

Air Pollutant Emissions

Air pollution emissions occur primarily during installation and operation due to combustion of diesel fuel and natural gas by generators, vessel engines, and equipment. Flaring is another source of air pollution emissions. Air emissions from the proposed activity are addressed in **Chapter 3.1.2**.

Presence of Structures

The presence of offshore structures, including noise and lights, can have impacts on marine life, including fishes, marine mammals, turtles, and birds. It is well known that offshore structures serve as artificial reefs (Reggio, 1987; LGL Ecological Research Associates, Inc. and Science Applications International Corporation, 1998). In addition, offshore drilling and production activities produce a broad array of sounds at frequencies and intensities that may be detected by marine mammals and sea turtles. Brightly lit offshore platforms may attract sea turtle hatchlings, which could be subject to increased predation by birds and fishes that are also attracted to offshore structures.

Vessel and Helicopter Traffic

Vessels will travel back and forth between the DP semisubmersible and FPU and the shore base in Port Fourchon, Louisiana. Helicopters will travel back and forth from the heliport in Port Fourchon, Louisiana. The boats will normally move to the project area via the most direct route. The helicopter will be used for transporting personnel and small supplies and will normally take the most direct route of travel between the shore base and the project area when air traffic and weather conditions permit. Vessel and helicopter traffic may startle or disturb birds, marine mammals, and turtles. There is also a small risk of a supply boat or crewboat striking a marine mammal or turtle.

Trash and Debris

Potential trash and debris sources include the DP semisubmersible and FPU, construction vessels, and transportation vessels. Ingestion of, or entanglement with, accidentally discarded debris can kill or injure marine mammals, turtles, and birds.

Accidents (Oil Spills)

A spill is unlikely and, historically, most spills from offshore operations have been small. The MMS (USDOI, MMS, 2007) used an average spill size of 5 bbl for small (<1,000 bbl) offshore spills.

The worst-case discharge is a crude oil spill of 21,000 barrels of oil per day which is estimated to be the volume of oil that could be released as a result of a well blowout and the loss of all storage and pipelines connected to the FPU. Blowouts are rare and usually do not result in a spill. Since 1998, four blowouts in the GOM have resulted in oil spills, with the amount of oil spilled ranging from <1 bbl to 200 bbl. There have been no spills ≥1,000 bbl from blowouts in the last 30 years (USDOI, MMS, 2003a). As a result of Hurricanes Katrina and Rita in 2005, there were a total of 125 spills of ≥1 bbl and 39 spills of ≥50 bbl.

Other potential spill sources during the life of this development project (5 years) would include a spill of liquid oil stored on the platform (approximately 1,850-bbl total storage capacity including flowlines on the facility), a spill of liquid oil stored on the semisubmersible rig (approximately 19,000 bbl total storage capacity), a spill of liquid oil stored on the associated vessels (capacity of the largest vessel is 2,000 bbl), or a spill from the associated oil flowlines or the export pipelines.

1.6. Regulatory Framework

Federal laws mandate the OCS leasing program and the environmental reviews for the actions proposed by operators that seek to explore and produce hydrocarbons from Federal waters. An explanation of applicable statutes and regulations that comprise the regulatory framework for OCS activity and this proposed action is contained in the Multisale EIS (USDOI, MMS, 2007) and is hereby incorporated by reference into this PEA.

2. Alternatives Considered

2.1. Nonapproval of the Proposal

If this alternative was selected, ERT would not be allowed to undertake the proposed activities. This alternative could prevent the exploration for hydrocarbons and could result in the potential loss of royalty income for the citizens of the United States. Considering this outcome and that minimal impacts are anticipated, this alternative was not selected for further analysis.

2.2. Approval with Existing Mitigation

The MMS's lease stipulations, OCS Operating Regulations, Notices to Lessees and Operators (NTL's), and other regulations and laws were identified throughout this environmental assessment as existing mitigation to minimize potential environmental effects associated with the proposed action. Since additional mitigations were identified to avoid or mitigate potential impacts with the proposed action, this alternative was not selected.

2.3. Approval with Existing and/or Added Mitigation

The MMS's lease stipulations, OCS Operating Regulations, NTL's, and other regulations and laws were identified throughout this environmental assessment as existing mitigation to minimize potential environmental effects associated with the proposed action. Approval of the proposal with existing and additional mitigation is the selected alternative. The following additional mitigation has been identified.

Mitigation 8.03 (Advisory)—H₂S Absent

> The area in which the proposed drilling operations are to be conducted is hereby classified as "H_2S absent," in accordance with 30 CFR 250.417(c). The location and depths of the planned wells are not expected to encounter an H_2S hazard. An H_2S Contingency Plan is not required to be submitted and approved by the MMS prior to ERT conducting the proposed activities. (8.03)

3. Descriptions and Impact Analyses of the Affected Resources

Chapter 3 describes the physical, biological, socioeconomic, and human resources in and adjacent to Grid 9, as well as within Green Canyon Blocks 236 and 237, that could be potentially affected by activities associated with the proposed Phoenix Project. The descriptions present environmental resources as they are now, thus providing baseline information for further analyses where potential impacts from future projects in Grid 9 are examined. Discussions in the Multisale EIS (USDOI, MMS, 2007) are hereby incorporated by reference into this PEA and are briefly summarized throughout this PEA.

3.1. Physical Resources

Descriptions of the following components of the physical environment are contained in Appendix A of the Multisale EIS (USDOI, MMS, 2007): (1) geologic and geographic setting; (2) physical oceanography; (3) meteorological conditions; and (4) existing OCS-related infrastructure. These discussions are hereby incorporated by reference into this PEA.

Physical environments in the CPA are characterized in Chapter 3.1 of the Multisale EIS (USDOI, MMS, 2007) and are hereby incorporated by reference into this PEA. Summaries of these resources follow and include water quality and air quality.

3.1.1. Water Quality

3.1.1.1. Coastal Waters

3.1.1.1.1. Description

A detailed description of the coastal water quality can be found in Chapter 3.1.2.1. of the Multisale EIS and are hereby incorporated reference. The following information is a summary of the impact analysis incorporated from the Multisale EIS (USDOI, MMS, 2007). Coastal water quality along Louisiana and Texas is relevant to the Phoenix Project. The identified service base for the drilling, completion, and production activities from the new and existing wells in Green Canyon Blocks 236, 237, 238, and 282 is located on the coast in Port Fourchon, Louisiana. Marine transportation to and from Green Canyon Blocks 236 and 237 would traverse coastal waters.

Water quality in coastal waters of the northern GOM is highly influenced by season. For example, salinity in open water near the coast may vary between 29 and 32 parts per thousand (ppt) during fall and winter but decline to 20 ppt during spring and summer due to increased runoff (USDOI, MMS, 2000a). Temperature, dissolved oxygen, and nutrient concentrations also vary seasonally.

Gulf Coast water quality was given a fair rating in the National Coastal Condition Report II (USEPA, 2004).

Population growth in coastal areas can result in a decline in water quality. Urban runoff is the leading source of contaminants that impair coastal water quality.

Vessels from the shipping and fishing industries, as well as recreational boaters, add contaminants to coastal water in the form of bilge water, liquid and solid waste, spills, and chemicals leached from antifouling paints. Many millions of cubic feet of sediments are moved each year in coastal areas as a result of channelization, dredging, spoil disposal, and other hydromodifications. Water quality may be affected by these activities because they can lead to saltwater intrusion, increased turbidity, and the release of contaminants.

3.1.1.1.2. Impact Analysis

Sources that originate upriver from the Mississippi River Delta, as well as coastal sources, contribute to water quality degradation in nearshore and offshore environments of the GOM. These sources can be broadly characterized as industrial, agricultural, or municipal and point or nonpoint sources.

A discussion of impacts to coastal water quality from OCS activity is provided in Chapters 4.1.3.4, 4.2.1.1.2, and 4.2.2.1.2 of the Multisale EIS (USDOI, MMS, 2007) and is hereby incorporated by reference into this PEA.

The impact-producing factors associated with drilling, completion, and production of the Phoenix Project in Green Canyon that could affect coastal water quality include (1) effluents from onshore support bases and OCS service vessels, such as sanitary and domestic wastes; (2) turbidity increases from vessel traffic; and (3) accidental spills of crude oil, diesel fuel, chemicals associated with production, or other materials from vessels in coastal waters. Water-based drilling muds and cuttings discharges, and produced-water discharges are impact-producing factors that originate and are discharged at the Phoenix Project, which is located approximately 91 mi (147 km) from the Louisiana coast and over 100 mi (160 km) from the Texas and Mississippi coasts. The discharges are regulated by USEPA and will not impact coastal waters.

Domestic and sanitary waste would be discharged from support vessels after the required treatment. The effects on coastal waters from the Phoenix Project would primarily occur in heavy traffic areas such as navigation corridors and turning basins at Port Fourchon, Louisiana, which is the onshore support base.

Service vessels that use navigation channels, turning basins, shallow harbors, and docking facilities could cause increases in water turbidity from mud that is resuspended by propeller wash. Dredging and spoil dumping carried out to maintain, deepen, or straighten navigation channels could also increase the turbidity of coastal waters. Actions specifically attributed to vessels supporting the Phoenix Project would have an insignificant impact.

The Phoenix Project is located approximately 91 mi (147 km) from the nearest Louisiana coastline. The distance of this project and the Green Canyon Blocks 236 and 237 infrastructure from coastal waters introduces lengthy spill travel times and tremendous dilution factors for any accidental spills of crude oil, diesel fuel, or other materials. Spills that affect coastal waters would tend to originate from pipelines leaks or severance or from vessels in transit to or from the coastal area. Spills that may occur in Green Canyon Blocks 236 and 237 present an extremely small likelihood of affecting coastal water resources. If a large spill (≥1,000 bbl) were to occur at the surface or originate from a well blowout, the oil would form a surface slick. Response efforts can recover or disperse some of the slick, and high surf could contribute to its break up while at sea. Weathering and evaporation of volatile organics can degrade a slick while at sea. Slicks existing for 10 days or more have a small chance to wash ashore.

Some wastes not permitted for offshore disposal are brought ashore for disposal or recycling and can present spill hazards if not handled properly. Although not all these waste types will be generated by the developmental drilling, completion, and production from the Green Canyon Blocks 236 and 237 wells covered by this DOCD, exploration and production waste (E&P waste) can include oil-based drilling fluids and drill cuttings, liquid wastes ("fracing" fluids, i.e., fluids forced into formations to fracture, dissolve cement, or prop open pore throats, emulsifiers, workover fluids, mud additives, etc.), and possibly well test solids and produced sand and are also transported across coastal waters to shore. These wastes are taken to transfer stations and on to State-regulated disposal locations in Texas and Louisiana.

Conclusion

No significant long-term impacts on coastal water quality would be expected from the proposed Phoenix Project. Because the proposed action would use existing onshore support bases, only the discharges from these support bases or service vessels would result in effects to coastal waters. The contribution by the proposed action to the level of these effects is expected to be very minor, transient, and not contribute significantly to the decline in coastal water quality. Spilled oil originating in coastal waters and attributable to the Phoenix Project would not be ≥1,000 bbl and is expected to be substantially recovered while still at sea.

3.1.1.1.3. Cumulative Analysis

Cumulative impacts on water quality include sources of pollutants that affect both coastal and offshore settings. Human sources in coastal waters include effluents, wastes, or surface runoff from varied urban, rural, and industrial sources. These sources include the following: (1) petrochemical industry (inclusive of OCS development and processing); (2) agriculture and animal processing; (3) agricultural and urban runoff; (4) municipal and recreational sewerage treatment; (5) marinas; (6) commercial fishing; (7) maritime shipping and cruise ships; (8) hydromodification activities; (9) wood processing, pulp, and paper mills; (10) recreational boating and fishing; (11) manufacturing activities; (12) accidental spills of oil, diesel fuel, or other material; and (13) atmospheric deposition of airborne contaminants onto the sea. Contaminants entering coastal waters can also be transported to offshore marine waters.

Human sources in offshore waters include effluents and discharges from fixed (e.g., mobile offshore drilling units (MODU's), semisubmersibles, and production platforms) and mobile sources (i.e., vessels of all types). Each fixed or mobile source has routine and permitted effluents and discharges. Fixed platforms and MODU's discharge (1) water-based muds and cuttings; (2) cuttings wetted with synthetic-based mud (SBM); (3) small quantities of wellbore cement and treatment, completion, and workover chemicals; (4) domestic and sanitary discharges; (5) produced water; (6) bilge, ballast, cooling, and desalinization unit water; and (7) deck wash.

Vessels such as OCS service boats and crewboats, freighters, tankers, barges, fishing boats, and cruise ships discharge (1) bilge, ballast, and cooling water; (2) domestic and sanitary discharges; and (3) deck wash. Both fixed and mobile sources can accidentally spill oil, diesel fuel, or other material, and trash and debris can be lost overboard despite handling requirements.

Worldwide, natural seeps from geologic formations release 4,200,000 bbl (1.8 x 10^8 gal) of oil into the oceans each year (NRC, 2003). Natural hydrocarbon seeps are the most significant source of oil entering Gulf waters. Relatively recent studies have suggested that seepage rates in the GOM are much higher than earlier estimates (NRC, 2003). Mitchell (2000) estimated that 500,000 bbl/yr of oil seeped into northern GOM waters (U.S. territorial waters); a figure NRC doubled to estimate seepage rates for the entire GOM. In the same range, if apportioned to the GOM, would be a estimate by MMS (USDOI, MMS, 2003b), which concluded that 1,700 bbl/day are released into all U.S. territorial waters each day by natural seeps (620,000 bbl/yr). The NRC (2003) estimated that an average of 980,000 bbl of oil enters the entire GOM each year from natural seeps (with a range of 560,000 to 1,400,000 bbl). This average amount is four times the volume of the 1989 *Exxon Valdez* spill (USDOC, NOAA, 1992) every year.

The NRC (2003) reports the annual contribution of oil in marine waters of North America (U.S. and Canada) from various human activities and natural sources. The NRC (2003) provided a best estimate that 1,820,000 bbl of petroleum enters North American marine waters (U.S. and Canada) each year. The majority of this amount is from natural seeps; approximately 1,120,000 bbl or 62 percent. The NRC (2003) has shown that the largest fraction of oil entering the water from all sources relates to the consumption of petroleum (33%) and that only 5 percent is related to the production or transportation of oil (including refining). Subtracting out the amount contributed by natural seeps, nearly 85 percent of the 627,700 bbl of oil entering North American marine waters each year from human activities comes from the following sources, in relative order: (1) land-based runoff and polluted rivers; (2) recreational boats and jet skis, particularly those with 2-cycle engines; (3) atmospheric deposition; and (4) jettisoned aircraft fuel (NRC, 2003). Approximately 9 percent of the total attributable to human activity comes from transportation, pipeline, or refining activity (NRC, 2003), and 3 percent comes from oil and gas exploration and production (NRC, 2003).

No irreversible or irretrievable impacts to the marine environment on a broad oceanic scale are caused by either natural seeps or accidental spills (NRC, 2003). Natural seeps have released oil into the GOM and the oceans of the world in all types of coastal and marine environments for millennia. Natural marine systems can accommodate rather substantial quantities of oil in the sea, apparently without much noticeable impact.

The incremental contribution of the proposed action's impacts to the cumulative impact on coastal water quality is negligible and likely undetectable among the other cumulative impacts.

3.1.1.2. Offshore Waters

3.1.1.2.1. Description

The water offshore of the Gulf coasts can be divided into two regions: the continental shelf and the slope (<1,000 ft or 305 m) and deep water (>1,000 ft or 305 m). The continental shelf off the modern Mississippi River Delta is narrow because of the outbuilding of sediment from the river onto the shelf. To the east and west the shelf broadens. Waters on the continental shelf and slope are heavily influenced by the Mississippi and Atchafalaya Rivers, the primary sources of freshwater, sediment, and pollutants from a huge drainage basin encompassing 55 percent of the continental U.S. (Murray, 1998). Lower salinities are characteristic nearshore where freshwater from the rivers mix with Gulf waters. While the average discharge from the Mississippi River exceeds the input of all other rivers along the Texas-Louisiana coast by a factor of 10, during low-flow periods the Mississippi River can have a flow less than all these rivers combined (Nowlin et al., 1998).

A zone of hypoxia on the Louisiana-Texas shelf is one of the largest areas of low oxygen in the world's coastal waters (Murray, 1998). Hypoxic conditions are caused by a seasonal stratified water column. The less dense and low-salinity water from the Mississippi River "floats" on top of denser, more saline water and creates a stratified water column. High nutrient loads in the river water enhance algae production and increase the amount of decaying organic matter accumulating at the sea bottom. Decay depletes oxygen in bottom waters to the point of hypoxia (<2 mg/l dissolved oxygen) while the oxygen content of near-surface water is at or near to saturation. The hypoxic oxygen levels are low enough to affect the abundance, health, and vitality of soft-bottom invertebrate faunas and bottom-dwelling fish. Under severe or prolonged conditions it can kill bottom fauna.

The presence or extent of a nepheloid layer at the sea bottom affects water quality on the shelf and slope. A nepheloid layer is a zone of suspended clay-sized particles that may play a role in transporting fine-grained sediment and contaminants from nearshore to offshore waters. The nepheloid layer can be thin and near bottom or very thick, depending on factors such as water depth, depth of water-column mixing, season, and sediment input. The shelf area is characterized by a bottom nepheloid layer and surface lenses of suspended particulates that originate from river outflow. Freshwater from the

18

Mississippi/Atchafalaya River systems may carry trace amounts of organic pollutants, including polynuclear aromatic hydrocarbons (PAH); herbicides such as atrazine, chlorinated pesticides, and polychlorinated biphenyls (PCB's); and trace inorganic (metals) pollutants.

The concentration of hydrocarbons in slope sediments (except in seep areas) is lower than concentrations reported for shelf and coastal sediments (Gallaway et al., 2003). In general, the CPA has higher levels of hydrocarbons in sediment, particularly those from terrestrial sources, than the WPA and Eastern Planning Area (EPA) (Gallaway and Kennicutt, 1988). Total organic carbon is also highest in the CPA. Hydrocarbons in sediments have been determined to influence biological communities of the Gulf slope, even when present in trace amounts (Gallaway and Kennicutt, 1988).

Hydrocarbon seeps are extensive throughout the continental slope and contribute hydrocarbons to the surface sediments and water column, especially in the CPA (Sassen et al., 1993a and b). Natural hydrocarbon seepage is considered to be a major source of petroleum into Gulf slope waters (Kennicutt et al., 1987; Gallaway et al., 2003), and the NRC (2003) considers seeps to be the predominant source. MacDonald et al. (1993) observed 63 individual seeps using remote-sensing and submarine observations. The NRC (2003) reported that estimates of the total volume of seeping oil in the GOM vary widely from 28,000 bbl/yr (MacDonald, 1998) to a range of between 280,000 and 700,000 bbl/yr (Mitchell et al., 1999). The NRC's own best estimate is an annual input of 980,000 bbl/yr for the entire Gulf (NRC, 2003), which is four times the volume of the *Exxon Valdez* spill per year (estimated to have been 260,000 bbl (NRC, 2003)). Clearly, natural seeps account for a large quantity of oil that enters Gulf waters each year from a phenomena occurring over geologic time scales. Seep oil is a natural component of Gulf water, and oil in the water is called a pollutant or contaminant only when introduced in large quantities in a small area over a short period of time.

In addition to hydrocarbon seeps, other fluids leak from the underlying sediments into the bottom water along the slope. These fluids have been identified to have three origins: (1) seawater trapped during the settling of sediments; (2) brine from dissolution of underlying salt diapirs; and (3) deep-seated formation waters (Fu and Aharon, 1998; Aharon et al., 2001).

Produced water (formation water) is the volumetrically largest waste stream from the oil and gas industry that enters Gulf waters. Produced water is commonly treated to separate free oil and is either injected back into the reservoir or discharged overboard according to NPDES permit limits (**Chapter 1.4**, Offshore Discharges and Waste Disposal). The NRC has estimated the quantity of oil in produced water entering the Gulf per year to be 473,000 bbl (NRC, 2003; Table D-8).

Green Canyon Blocks 236 and 237 are entirely in deep water, for which limited information is available on water quality. Generally, the water quality in deep water could be considered significantly better than that of the coastal waters (USDOI, MMS, 2007). Water at depths >1,400 m (4,593 ft) is relatively homogeneous with respect to temperature, salinity, and oxygen (Nowlin, 1972; Pequegnat, 1983; Gallaway et al., 1988). Offshore Texas, Louisiana, and Alabama show detectable levels of petroleum hydrocarbons, likely from natural seeps (USDOI, MMS, 1997 and 2000b). Pequegnat (1983) pointed out the importance of water-column mixing and flush time for the GOM. Oxygen in deep water must originate from the surface and be mixed into deep water by some mechanism, but the time for turnover or the mechanism by which oxygen replenishment takes place in the deep GOM is essentially unknown.

Deepwater sediments, with the exception of barium concentrations in the vicinity of previous drilling, do not appear to contain elevated levels of metal contaminants (USDOI, MMS, 1997 and 2000b). Reported total hydrocarbons, including biogenic (e.g., from plankton and other biological sources) hydrocarbons, in sediments collected from the Gulf slope range from 5 to 86 ng/g (Kennicutt et al., 1987). Petroleum hydrocarbons, including aromatic hydrocarbons (<5 ppb), were present at all sites sampled.

The MMS studied the effect of exploration and development at four drilling sites located in water depths greater than 1,000 m (3,280 ft) (CSA, 2006). The sampling design called for before and after exploratory or development drilling and captured the drilling-related changes that occur in sediments and sediment pore water. Samples were collected from near- and far-field locations in the interval between exploratory drilling and development drilling and again after development wells were drilled. The Garden Banks sample locations were about 70 mi (113 km) west of the Phoenix Project in similar water depths. Three exploratory wells had been drilled, and barite was elevated in nearly all near-field sample stations. Some concentrations of metals associated with barite were also elevated at near-field stations above far-field concentrations. Total PAH concentrations in the near-field sediments ranged from 194 to

3,470 ng/g following exploratory drilling and from 142 to 431 ng/g a year later and after the drilling of five development wells.

3.1.1.2.2.   Impact Analysis

The impact-producing factors associated with proposed Phoenix Project and commencement of production in Green Canyon that could affect offshore water quality include (1) degradation of GOM offshore waters from coastal activity, runoff, and riverine inputs; (2) discharges during the drilling of wells; (3) discharges during production, (4) bottom disturbances related to the installation of the subsea manifold and placement of the new or replacement of the additional hurricane-damaged flowlines and umbilicals and accidental spills of crude oil, diesel fuel, chemicals or other materials from vessels in offshore waters. A discussion of impacts to offshore water quality from OCS activity is provided in Chapters 4.1.3.4, 4.2.1.1.2, and 4.2.2.1.2 of the Multisale EIS (USDOI, MMS, 2007) and is hereby incorporated by reference into this PEA.

Operations

Water depths in Green Canyon Blocks 236 and 237 range from 1,600 to 2,400 ft (488 to 732 m). These deep marine waters and environments would be most directly affected by the proposed Phoenix Project activities. Drilling activities will be conducted from a DP semisubmersible drilling rig. Production will be conducted from a dynamically positioned FPU with no sediment disturbance from moorings, anchors, or pipeline placement. Sediment disturbances will result from the replacement of the subsea flowlines, umbilicals and manifold. A range of effluents and wastes would be discharged overboard from the proposed Phoenix Project. Overboard discharges and wastes intended from the project are shown in the wastes and discharge tables (**Tables A-1 and A-2**, respectively). The types and discharge rates will be in accordance with USEPA NPDES General Permit GMG 290000 for USEPA Region 6, or an individual NPDES permit if one is secured by ERT and its partners. Wastes destined for onshore disposal or recycling pose no potential impacts to affected resources unless spilled.

A total of six new development wells would be drilled. Water-based drilling fluid (WBF) would be used. The DOCD estimates the use of 10,000 bbl of WBF per well and the discharge of 2,500 bbl per well of water-based drilling mud containing barite per well. The MMS estimates about 2,000-3,000 bbl of WBF cuttings per well. Five existing wells would be put back on line.

Sanitary and domestic waste would be produced on the semisubmersible at rates of 20 gal/person/day and 30 gal/person/day, respectively. These discharges are treated to meet USEPA discharge requirements. Discharge would occur daily. Water would be impacted by the introduction of suspended solids and biochemical oxygen demand (BOD) matter. Offshore waste and discharge tables for the Phoenix Project are included in **Appendix A**.

Accidental Events

The failure or disconnect of a riser system could result in the release of some or all of the fluid in the annuli. Riser system failures and disconnects, though not common, have occurred in the past (USDOI, MMS, 2000b and 2003c).

No blowouts resulting in spills ≥1,000 bbl are projected as a result of drilling associated with the Phoenix Project based on historical trends in the GOM (**Appendix B**). Based upon historical spill rates and the anticipated volumes over the life of the Phoenix Project, it is projected that spills that occur from the Phoenix Project would be few (if any).

Conclusion

No significant long-term impacts on offshore water quality would be expected from the proposed Phoenix Project. Near-bottom water quality would be affected by increased turbidity and disturbed substrates during the period of drilling subsea production equipment placement. Any effects from the elevated turbidity would be short term, localized, and reversible. Small numbers of bottom-dwelling invertebrates may be killed or adversely impacted.

Impacts on offshore water quality from the operational discharges that would be expected to result from the Phoenix Project are insignificant because of (1) existing environmental regulations, (2) great water depth, (3) distance of the project from the coast, (4) spill transit times, and (5) dilution factors. An accidental oil spill would affect water quality at the surface (top few meters or feet of the water column). Operator-initiated activities to contain and clean up an oil spill would begin as soon as possible after an event. Small quantities of unrecovered oil would weather and largely biodegrade within 2 weeks.

3.1.1.2.3. Cumulative Analysis

The sources identified in Chapter 3.1.1 of the Multisale EIS (USDOI, MMS, 2007) contribute to cumulative water quality degradation in offshore waters. Spills of oil, diesel fuel, and other materials may occur from vessels transporting crude oil and petroleum products; from vessels involved in commercial fishing, freight, or passenger transport; and from OCS operations. Well blowouts can disturb the bottom, increase turbidity, and put oil into the sea. Should one of these blowouts occur, localized, short-term changes in water quality would be expected. Cumulative impacts would be negligible.

Bottom-area disturbances resulting from non-OCS sources are not expected in Green Canyon Blocks 236 and 237 water depths. Cumulative impacts are negligible.

Daily operational discharges to offshore waters occur from vessels moving through Gulf waters and from MODU's and production facilities (Chapters 3.1.1.1.2 and 3.1.1.2.2 of the Multisale EIS (USDOI, MMS, 2007)). The discharge of drilling fluid, cuttings, and produced water are the main effluents from oil and gas exploration, development, and production operations. The contaminant deposition and accumulation rate on the sea bottom from discharges is primarily dependent on the water depth and current strength. Sediment contaminants from OCS discharges may occur from several hundred to several thousand meters or feet from the discharge point depending on the volumes discharged. Biological responses to contaminant levels retained in bottom sediments are not expected to be detectable beyond a couple hundred meters or feet, and toxic effects to the benthos would be localized, limited to within a hundred meters or feet of the discharge, and of a relatively small magnitude. Toxic effects beyond 100 m (328 ft) should be controlled through the USEPA's NPDES permit requirements.

Well blowouts can resuspend fine-grained sediment in the water to increase turbidity. The rapid accumulation of sediment (or cuttings if well drilling is part of the development project) on the sea bottom that are thicker than 30 cm (1 ft) would be lethal for all sessile and most motile invertebrates (Frey, 1975; Basan et al., 1978; Ekdale et al., 1984). An accumulation rate of this type would not be expected in most deepwater development projects, and most soft-bottom, motile invertebrates would have a chance to react and move. Diluted and discharged slowly over large areas, these wastes contribute in a very small way to the degradation of offshore water quality. As a result, cumulative impacts are negligible.

3.1.2. Air Quality

3.1.2.1. Description

Green Canyon Blocks 236 and 237 are located west of 87.5° W. longitude and hence fall under MMS's jurisdiction for enforcement of the Clean Air Act. The air over the OCS water is not classified, but it is presumed to be better than the National Ambient Air Quality Standards (NAAQS) for all criteria pollutants. The Phoenix Project in Green Canyon Blocks 236 and 237 is located approximately 91 mi (145 km) south of Terrebonne Parish, Louisiana, an area that is in attainment of the NAAQS for CO, NO_x, SO_x, and PM and that, for prevention of significant deterioration (PSD) purposes, is classified as a Class II area.

The influence to onshore air quality is dependent upon meteorological conditions and air pollution emitted from operational activities. The pertinent meteorological conditions regarding air quality are the wind speed and direction, the atmospheric stability, and the mixing height (which govern the dispersion and transport of emissions). The typical synoptic wind flow for Green Canyon Blocks 236 and 237 are driven by the clockwise circulation around the Bermuda High, resulting in a prevailing southeasterly to southerly flow, which is conducive to transporting emissions toward shore. However, superimposed upon this synoptic circulation are smaller meso-scale wind flow patterns, such as the land/sea breeze phenomenon. In addition, there are other synoptic scale patterns that occur periodically, namely tropical cyclones, and mid-latitude frontal systems. Because of the routine occurrence of these various conditions, the winds blow from all directions in the area of concern (Florida A&M University, 1988).

3.1.2.2. Impact Analysis

Air quality would be affected in the immediate vicinity of the drilling and completion operations, service vessels, and aircraft. The cumulative impact from emissions for this DOCD will not exceed MMS's exemption levels. The drilling activities are not expected to significantly affect onshore air quality. The distance from Green Canyon Blocks 236 and 237 to any PSD Class I air quality area such as the Breton National Wildlife Refuge is >200 km (124 mi). Port Fourchon, Laforuche Parish, Louisiana, the location of the service base, is in attainment for ozone (USDOI, MMS, 2007).

Air quality could be affected in the event of spilled oil. The volatile organic compounds (VOC), which would escape to the atmosphere from a surface slick, are precursors to photochemically produced ozone. A spike in VOC's could contribute to a corresponding spike in ozone, especially if the release were to occur on a hot sunny day in a NO_2-rich environment. The corresponding onshore area is in nonattainment for ozone. However, due to the distance from shore, the project is not expected to have any impacts on onshore air quality including nonattainment areas. If a fire occurs, particulate and combustible emissions will be released in addition to the VOC's.

Conclusion

No significant long-term impacts on air quality would be expected from the proposed Phoenix Project. The air quality in the immediate vicinity of the proposed activities would be affected by the projected emissions. The distance between Green Canyon Blocks 236 and 237 and the shoreline introduces tremendous dilution factors for point-source emissions in Green Canyon Blocks 236 and 237. No special mitigation, monitoring, or reporting requirements apply to this project.

3.1.2.3. Cumulative Analysis

Cumulative impacts on air quality within the offshore area would come primarily from sources generated outside Green Canyon Blocks 236 and 237 and include emissions from industrial plants, power generation, and urban transportation. The location of Green Canyon Blocks 236 and 237 is far removed from coastal populations or industrial activity. The OCS activity that takes place in Green Canyon Blocks 236 and 237 is >90 mi (144 km) from shore and would not affect the overall quality of air over the Louisiana coast.

3.2 BIOLOGICAL RESOURCES

3.2.1. Sensitive Coastal Resources

Sensitive coastal environmental resources in the Central Gulf are characterized in Chapter 3.2.1 of the Multisale EIS (USDOI, MMS, 2007) and are hereby incorporated by reference into this PEA. Summaries of these resources follow and include (1) coastal barrier beaches and associated dunes and (2) wetlands.

The impact-producing factors associated with the proposed development and production of the Phoenix Project in Green Canyon Blocks 236 and 237 that could affect coastal barrier beaches and associated dunes, and wetlands include (1) oil spills from blowouts or vessel collisions, (2) chemical and drilling fluid spills, and (3) oil-spill response and cleanup. Of these, oil spills represent a high consequence and low-probability accidental event. Chapters 4.2.1.1.3 and 4.2.2.1.3 (Impacts on Sensitive Coastal Environments) of the Multisale EIS (USDOI, MMS, 2007) contain a discussion of impacts from OCS activity on coastal barrier beaches and associated dunes and wetlands and are hereby incorporated by reference into this PEA.

No blowouts would be expected as a result of well completions, workovers, or hydrocarbon production associated with the proposed Phoenix Project, based on historical trends in the GOM (**Table B-1**). Spills that occur from development and production activity would be few (if any), volumetrically small, and be located near project activities in Green Canyon Blocks 236 and 237.

Table B-4 indicates Gulfwide oil-spill occurrence rates. The statistics show that there have been numerous spills of >1 but <50 bbl but very few spills ≥1,000 bbl for all OCS operations per billion barrels of oil handled. A blowout is the only accident category that could yield a spill ≥1,000 bbl over the 5-year life cycle of the Phoenix Field production. The probability of a blowout is small, less than 1 in 100,000, and the combined probability of a spill ≥1,000 bbl making landfall in Louisiana or adjacent states would be extremely small (<0.5%).

Spills occurring in the deepwater environment of Grid 9 would not be large enough to enable them to persist long enough in the marine environment before weathering processes significantly degrade the spill before it makes landfall. The transport time would allow a slick to weather, dissolve, and disperse while still in the marine environment. If a spill occurs at sea, mechanical cleanup is assumed to collect up to 10 percent of the spilled oil and approximately 30 percent is assumed to be chemically dispersed, further reducing the overall probability and severity of spills that may enter coastal waters and make landfall. Because landfall of spilled oil, diesel fuel, drilling fluids, or chemicals is highly unlikely from the proposed activities, the potential impacts from spill landfall (i.e., response and cleanup activities on coastal barrier beaches and associated dunes and wetlands) would not be expected to occur.

Oil-spill response activity is governed by area contingency plans authorized by the Oil Pollution Act of 1990 and coordinated by the U.S. Coast Guard (USCG). These plans specify response procedures, priorities, and appropriate countermeasures for local coastal resources. The cleanup of slicks that come to rest in wetland areas or protected waters (0-1.5 m or 0-5 ft deep) may be performed using "john" boats, booms, anchors, and skimmers mounted on boats or shore vehicles. Oil-spill cleanup personnel in water shallower than about 1 m (3 ft) may simply wade through the water to complete their tasks. Trampling by foot traffic, swamp buggies, and cleanup equipment can cause damage to sensitive coastal resources by working oil more deeply into the sediments so that it is less available for dissolution, oxidation, or microbial degradation.

The loss of sensitive coastal environments from subsidence due to fluid withdrawal, dredging to maintain channels, flood control projects, and channelization can occur (USDOI, MMS, 2007; Chapter 4.5.3). Insofar as the oil and gas industry on the OCS is one of many industrialized uses of coastal waters, the incremental contribution of the proposed action to the cumulative impacts on sensitive coastal resources is expected to be very small.

3.2.1.1. Coastal Barrier Beaches and Associated Dunes

3.2.1.1.1. Description

The description, physical location, and formative processes that create the various coastal beaches and barrier island complexes are described in Chapter 3.2.1.1 of the Multisale EIS (USDOI, MMS, 2007). A description of integrated shoreline environments, the barrier islands, and the dune zones that comprise and delineate the various vegetated habitats along these mainland and barrier beaches can also be found in Chapter 3.2.1.1 of the Multisale EIS (USDOI, MMS, 2007); therefore, the discussion that follows hereby incorporates by reference the Multisale EIS and briefly summarizes the pertinent features of these resources in relation to their ability to allow, minimize, or neutralize the impact-producing factors associated with the proposed action. In addition, the post-hurricane condition of these island and beach resources, along with their integral protective features, will be described.

Each of the barriers is either high profile or low profile depending on the elevations and morphology of the island (Morton et al., 2004). The height and continuity of these elevations determine the ability of the barriers to withstand storm surge flooding and overwash. The Louisiana coastal barrier beaches and associated dunes that occur along this area of the GOM are typically composed of sandy beaches that are divided into several interrelated environments composed of a shore face, foreshore, and backshore. The Louisiana barrier island beaches are in constant flux as a result of the sediment source, composition, and the wave and wind climate in the vicinity of the islands. Those remaining Louisiana barrier islands located farther to the west are regressive in nature (island migration is more seaward), and the shorelines of these island formations are characterized by (1) wider and higher profiles, (2) well-vegetated dunes, and (3) few, if any, wash-over channels (USDOI, MMS, 2007). Thick accumulations of sand may form parallel ridges, such as those that typify the Chenier Plain of western coastal Louisiana. Both transgressive and regressive shorelines are important ecologically. Barrier islands, particularly vegetated ones with freshwater and/or saltwater pools, may serve as habitat for a wide variety of animal life, especially birds. In general, most of the Louisiana barrier island chain is moving landward, thereby increasing the vulnerability of the Louisiana coastline to storm surge along with the associated wetlands loss.

Hurricane Katrina in August 2005 caused severe erosion and landloss for the coastal barrier islands of the deltaic plain. The eye of Hurricane Katrina passed directly over the 50-mi (80-km) Chandeleur Island chain. Aerial surveys conducted by the U.S. Geological Survey on September 1, 2005, show that these islands were heavily damaged by the storm (USDOI, GS, 2005). Initial estimates suggest that Hurricane Katrina reduced the Chandeleur Islands by one-half of their pre-storm land area (USDOC, NOAA/NMFS, 2007). Although barrier islands and shorelines have some capacity to regenerate over time, the process is very slow and often incomplete. With each passing storm, the size and resiliency of these areas can be diminished, especially when major storms occur within a short time period. Hurricane Katrina was the fifth hurricane to impact the Chandeleur Island chain in the past 8 years. The other storms were Hurricanes Georges (1998), Lili (2002), Ivan (2004), and Dennis (2005).

Grand Isle was also heavily damaged by Hurricane Katrina. Although Hurricane Katrina made landfall more than 50 mi (80 km) to its east, Grand Isle received extremely high winds and a 12- to 20-ft (4- to 6-m) storm surge that caused tremendous structural damage to most of the island's camps, homes, and businesses (Louisiana Sea Grant, 2005). Hurricane Rita in September 2005 severely impacted the shoreface and beach communities of Cameron Parish in southwest Louisiana. Some small towns in this area have no standing structures remaining. A storm surge approaching 20 ft (6 m) caused beach erosion and overwash that flattened coastal dunes, depositing sand and debris well into the backing marshes. Barrier beaches and dune environments are further characterized in Chapter 3.2.1.1 of the Multisale EIS (USDOI, MMS, 2007).

In summary, the barrier islands from Texas to Florida (i.e., the WPA, CPA, and EPA) incurred some type of damage from the combination of Hurricanes Katrina and Rita and, in some cases, in combination with Hurricanes Wilma and Ivan as well. While Louisiana barrier islands incurred most of the damage, all of the areas experienced varying degrees of erosion, land and vegetation loss, loss in elevation or beach profile and, in some cases, movement toward shore as a result of the previous highly active hurricane season. The resulting changes in elevation and island profiles reduce the ability of these features to provide the pre-storm coastal protection to the mainland beaches and wetlands. While these barriers can rebuild to some extent naturally over time, it is the intent of both Federal and State coastal restoration projects, such as the Coastal Wetlands Planning, Protection, and Restoration Act, the Louisiana Coastal Restoration Program, and the Coastal Impact Assistance Program to assist in these barrier island restorations.

3.2.1.1.2. Impact Analysis

The impact-producing factors associated with the proposed action that could affect coastal barrier beaches and associated dunes include support for the construction from onshore facilities; vessel traffic; and oil spills from blowouts or vessel collisions, spill response, and cleanup. No nearshore pipeline emplacement or new pipeline corridors are needed as a result of this proposed action. The impact-producing factors described above are discussed in Chapter 4.1.1 of the Multisale EIS in (USDOI, MMS, 2007) and are hereby incorporated by reference into this PEA. Site-specific analyses of potential impacts to resources are described in this Chapter. The subregional oil-spill response plan is discussed in **Appendix B**.

It is assumed all offshore coastal spills would contact land and proximate resources. Most inshore spills resulting from the proposed action would occur from barge, pipeline, and storage tank accidents involving transfer operations, leaks, and pipeline breaks, which are remote from coastal barrier beaches. For a barge or pipeline accident in State or Federal offshore waters to affect a coastal barrier beach, the accident would need to occur on a coastal barrier beach or associated dune, or in the vicinity of a tidal inlet.

During well and subset well installation there are expected to be slight increases in the number of vessel transits to and from support bases and fabrication yards, resulting in minor incremental impacts to channels and coastal erosion rates. Given the limited number of vessels required and the relatively short timeframe for each phase of installation activity, such impacts are short term and extremely localized. The significance of these incremental increases in impacts varies depending upon the location of the transport vessel destination, which in this case is Port Fourchon, Louisiana.

Vessel traffic through channels and in close proximity to coastal barrier islands has been shown to move considerably more bottom sediment than tidal currents, thus increasing coastal and barrier island erosion rates. The incremental increases in channel and coastal erosion associated with increased vessel traffic can be expected to be more significant in those coastal barrier island or beach locations that are currently undergoing transgression. The erodability of some of the coastal barrier islands off of Louisiana and Mississippi has increased due to the hurricane-induced erosion and the removal or die off of the wetland vegetation. However, given the level of other tanker and vessel traffic using Gulf ports, impacts on coastal environments from the proposed oil transport operation is considered to range from negligible to adverse but not significant, depending upon the nature of adjacent coastal environments.

There are no new navigation channels planned; however, there is potential for maintenance dredging of existing channels to assure appropriate depths for the shuttle tankers. This dredged material will be beneficially used either for wetland creation or beach restoration.

While offshore oil spills could pose problems for beaches and nearshore barrier islands, these coastal features would be the most susceptible to inshore spills associated with vessel collisions, offloading, or pipeline breaks. Due to the proximity of the proposed work to the nearest coastal barrier islands (85-90 mi or 137-145 km), the oil is expected to be sufficiently weathered such that the toxicity of the oil reaching the barrier or mainland beaches would be little to none. The combined probability of a spill greater than or equal to 1,000 bbl occurring from the proposed activities and contacting shoreline resources within 30 days from the Phoenix Project launch area is <0.5 percent. Given the distance of the proposed action from shore and the shore base (91-105 mi or 146-169 km), spills are expected to weather and would generally not reach shore. Given this low probability of a spill occurring as a result of the proposed action and contacting a coastal barrier beach, the risk of spills from the Phoenix production site to coastal barrier beaches in the Gulf of Mexico is low.

The likelihood of contact of spilled materials with coastal barrier beaches and associated dunes is dependent on the meteorological and current conditions at the time of the spill and on the quantity and location of the spill. In coastal Louisiana, the heights of dune lines range from 1.6 to 4 ft (0.5 to 1.3 m) above mean high tide levels. For spilled oil to move onto beaches or across dunes, strong southerly winds must persist for an extended time prior to or immediately after the spill approaches the shoreline to elevate water levels. Strong winds would accelerate oil-slick dispersal, spreading, and weathering, thereby reducing impact severity at a landfall site. Any coastal barrier beach or associated dune contacted by a spill associated with the proposed activity is very unlikely, except during abnormally high water levels, such as might occur during a hurricane. A study in Texas showed that oil disposal on sand and vegetated sand dunes had little deleterious effects on the existing vegetation or on the recolonization of the oiled sands by plants (Webb, 1988). Oil or its components that remain in the sand after cleanup may be (1) released periodically when storms and high tides resuspend or flush beach sediments, (2) decomposed by biological activity, or (3) volatilized and dispersed during hot or sunny days.

The cleanup impacts of these spills could result in a short-term (up to 2 years) adjustment in beach profiles and configurations as a result of sand removal and disturbance during cleanup operations. Some contact to the lower areas of sand dunes is expected. These contacts would not result in significant destabilization of the dunes. The long-term stressors to coastal barrier beach communities caused by the physical effects and chemical toxicity of an oil spill may lead to decreased primary production, plant dieback, and hence further erosion.

In summary on a local basis, oil spills from the Phoenix operations could produce either adverse (but not significant) or extended (but not irreversible) impacts on coastal barrier beaches, depending upon spill size, the nature of the oil coming ashore (e.g., highly vs. lightly weathered), and the location and characteristics of the coastal barrier beach. Impacts may be long term, depending upon spill location and the relative position of sensitive resources. However, the combined probability of a spill >1,000 bbl contacting coastal barrier beaches and associated dunes in any county or parish within 30 days is extremely low (≤.5%). Modeled locations indicate smaller spills are not predicted to reach these beaches or the associated wetlands.

3.2.1.1.3   Cumulative Analysis

Barrier beaches along coastal Louisiana and Texas have experienced severe erosion and landward retreat (marine transgression) because of natural processes enhanced by human activities. Mississippi, Alabama, and Florida have also experienced beach erosion and shoreline depletion in varying degrees as a result of recent hurricanes, i.e., Hurricanes Katrina, Rita, Ivan, and Wilma (USDOC, NMFS, 2007). The cumulative effect of these barrier island losses will continue as future tropical storms and hurricanes approach these coasts and further degrade these barriers.

Impact-producing factors from non-OCS activity that contribute to coastal barrier beach and dune erosion, or conversion to another environment, include (1) levee construction and stabilization structures for channels and beaches; (2) natural processes such as hurricanes, erosion, and subsidence; (3)

recreational vehicle use on dunes and beaches; (4) recreational and commercial development; and (5) removal of coastal vegetation. Deterioration of Gulf barrier beaches is expected to continue in the future.

The scenario of impact-producing factors related to OCS activity may include pipeline emplacement, and vessel-induced erosion. Accidental impact producing factors include oil spills and the resultant beach cleanup. However, due to the distance of the proposed OCS activity from shore, the absence of pipeline landfalls, and the minimal shuttle-tanker trips, only the following impact-producing factors could potentially affect the coastal barrier beaches and associated dunes. These impact-producing factors would include the minimal (<5% chance) potential of beach oiling from oil spills and the minimal potential for vessel-related erosion. Additional OCS activities in the foreseeable future could include the need for pipeline emplacement, onshore facilities, and increased supply vessel and tanker support for potential increases in the construction of floating production, storage, and offloading systems in the GOM.

The incremental contribution of the proposed action's impacts to the cumulative impact on coastal barrier beaches and associated dunes is negligible and likely undetectable among the other cumulative impacts. However, if future pipeline installations are necessary, avoidance procedures for pipeline emplacement near coastal barrier beaches and associated dunes have been included in "conditioned permits" required by the Corps of Engineers. These procedures assure that pipeline activities near these sensitive beaches are placed under the islands and beaches using indirect drilling techniques, or the pipeline routing is planned to avoid these sensitive areas.

3.2.1.2. *Wetlands*

3.2.1.2.1 Description

A detailed description of the coastal wetlands can be found in Chapter 3.2.1.2 of the Multisale EIS and are hereby incorporated by reference into this PEA. The following information is a summary of the impact analysis incorporated from the Multisale EIS (USDOI, MMS, 2007). Wetland habitats found along the Central and Western Gulf Coast include fresh, intermediate, brackish, and saline marshes; mud and sand flats; and forested wetlands of mangrove swamps, cypress-tupelo swamps, and bottomland hardwoods. Coastal wetland habitats occur as bands around waterways and as broad expanses. Saline and brackish habitats support sharply delineated, segregated stands of single plant species. Fresh and very low salinity environments support more diverse and mixed communities of plants. The plant species that occur in greatest abundance vary greatly around the Gulf. These wetlands are high in organic activity, producing needed nutrients to adjacent waters and marshes that, in turn, provide habitat for a great number and wide diversity of invertebrates, fish, reptiles, birds, and mammals. These wetlands also provide nutrient recycling and detrital production so important in making these areas particularly important as nursery grounds for many fish and shellfish juveniles that, in turn, support a thriving fishing industry. Louisiana's coastal wetlands support more than two-thirds of the wintering waterfowl population of the Mississippi Flyway, including 20-25 percent of North America's puddle duck population. Louisiana's coastal region also supports the largest fur harvest in North America (Olds, 1984).

During 1997, the area of interest in Louisiana contained about 708,570 ha (1,750,915 ac) of coastal wetlands. About 32,570 ha (80, 482 ac) of this were freshwater marsh and forests, 175,560 ha (433,818 ac) were intermediate salinity marsh, and 207,440 ha (512,595 ac) were brackish marsh (Louisiana Dept. of Wildlife and Fisheries, 1997). Presumably, the remaining 293,000 ha (724,018 ac) were saline marsh. These wetlands largely occur as broad expanses. More recent information is provided below by geographic area, including recent land change as a result of Hurricanes Katrina and Rita. The most notable was the 217 mi^2 (562 km^2) of Louisiana's coastal lands that were transformed to water after Hurricanes Katrina and Rita (Barras, 2006). Based on the analysis of the latest satellite imagery (Barras, 2007a and b) approximately 82 mi^2 (212 km^2) of new water areas were in areas primarily impacted by Hurricane Katrina (Mississippi River Delta Basin, Breton Sound Basin, Pontchartrain Basin, and Pearl River Basin), whereas 117 mi^2 (256 km^2) were in areas primarily impacted by Hurricane Rita (Calcasieu/Sabine Basin, Mermentau Basin, Teche/Vermillion Basin, Atchafalaya Basin, and Terrebonne Basin). Barataria Basin contained new water areas caused by both hurricanes, resulting in some 18 mi^2 (46.6 km^2) of new water areas.

These new water areas represent landlosses caused by the direct removal of wetlands. They also indicate transitory changes in water area caused by remnant flooding, removal of aquatic vegetation, scouring of marsh vegetation, and water-level variation attributed to normal tidal and meteorological variation between satellite images. It was noted (Barras, 2006) that permanent losses cannot be estimated until several growing seasons have passed and the transitory impacts of the hurricanes are minimized. It is, however, too early to estimate the actual overall marsh loss.

3.2.1.2.2. Impact Analysis

The primary impact-producing activities associated with routine activities for the proposed action that could affect wetlands include maintenance of existing navigation channels, vessel traffic-related erosion, disposal of OCS-related wastes, and use of support infrastructure in these coastal areas. Other potential impacts that are indirectly associated with OCS oil and gas activities are wake erosion resulting from navigation traffic, levee construction that prevents necessary sedimentary processes, sediment management structures (i.e., groins, jetties, and breakwaters), saltwater intrusion that changes the hydrology leading to unfavorable conditions for wetland vegetation, and vulnerability to storm damage from eroded wetlands. There are no new onshore facilities proposed for the proposed action at this stage of planning. There are currently disposal sites designated for OCS-related waste products as well as oil and gas support facilities located in the coastal wetlands that are capable of supporting existing activity in addition to that projected for the current exploration and production area. Due to the expected zero new pipeline landfalls from the proposed action and proposed use of existing processing facilities, no further expansion of either of the types of facilities should involve wetland expansions.

The addition of the proposed routine activities associated with the inclusion of the current project would have minimal to no direct effect on the coastal wetlands because the activities are 91 and 105 mi (146 and 169 km) from the nearest shoreline and shore base, respectively. The potential for indirect impacts may exist due to the initial needs for shore-based supply vessel support. Only a slight increase in vessel traffic is expected to occur but vessel size may increase due to supply needs and open-sea conditions. Transport vessels involved with the project consist of crewboats and work boats, each making no more than two trips per week. Helicopter trips are also expected to minimally increase with approximately three trips/week. Neither of the increases in support activity would require an expansion of onshore base support and, therefore, would not directly impact coastal wetlands. Port Fourchon is projected to be the primary base of onshore support operations and can be accessed by an armored channel. Since the vessel support will be using primarily armored coastal channels as well as existing offshore channels and sea lanes, vessel-related erosion should be minimal and the need for channel maintenance should not significantly increase as a result of the proposed activity.

The primary accidental impact-producing factors with the potential to affect the coastal wetlands are generally oil spills and, most specifically the coastal and inland spills resulting from vessel collisions or pipeline breaks adjacent to the coastal wetlands. While there is potential for accidental offshore spills affecting the coastal wetlands, the proximity of the lease site (91-105 mi; 146-169 km) to the nearest coast plus the probable weathered condition of the oil that may reach the shoreline minimizes the impact of these types of spills. Barrier islands can provide protection or reduce the severity of an oil spill by intercepting the spill before it reaches the wetlands located either behind (on mainland shore) or within the interior of the islands. Due to the lower post-hurricane (Hurricanes Katrina and Rita) elevations of the barrier islands along the Louisiana coast and to some extent the Texas coas,t there is now a greater chance of spilled oil reaching mainland shores (USDOC, NOAA/NMFS, 2007).

Trajectories of an offshore oil spill and the probability of it impacting a land segment have been projected using the MMS Oil-Spill Risk Analysis Model as described in **Appendix B**. The combined risk of a spill occurring and contacting Louisiana or Texas coastal counties and parishes within 3-30 days was <0.5%. There are concerns that offshore spills may contribute to wetland damage; however, due to the distance of the proposed action offshore, the possibility of spills reaching coastal wetlands with the toxicity to significantly impact the coastal wetlands is low. The toxicity of the spilled oils is greatly reduced or eliminated by weathering and wave action. The works of several investigators (Webb et al., 1981 and 1985; Alexander and Webb, 1983 and 1987; Lytle, 1975; Delaune et al., 1979; Fischel et al., 1989) evaluated the effects of potential spills to area wetlands. For wetlands along the central Louisiana coast, the critical oil concentration is assumed to be 1.0 L/m^2 of marsh. Concentrations above this would result in longer term effects to wetland vegetation, including some plant mortality and landloss. Concentrations less than this may cause diebacks for one growing season or less, depending upon the concentration and the season during which contact occurs. Chapter 4.3 of the Multisale EIS has a complete discussion of oil spills, the various impacting factors, and risk analysis; Chapter 4.4.3.2 of the Multisale EIS specifically addresses the types and severity of wetland impacts.

The fate and behavior of oil spills, availability and adequacy of oil-spill containment and cleanup technologies, oil-spill cleanup strategies, impacts of various oil-spill cleanup methods, effects of weathering on oil spills, toxicological effects of fresh and weathered oil, air pollution associated with spilled oil, and short-term and long-term impacts of oil on wetlands are additional accidental concerns. Offshore oil spills resulting from the proposed action are not expected to damage significantly any wetlands along the Gulf Coast. However, if an inland oil spill related to the proposed action occurs, some impact to wetland habitat would be expected. Although the probability of occurrence is low, the greatest threat to wetland habitat is from an inland spill resulting from a vessel accident or pipeline rupture. While a resulting slick may cause minor impacts to wetland habitat, the equipment and personnel used to clean up a slick over the impacted area may generate the greatest impacts to the area. Associated foot traffic may work oil farther into the sediment than would otherwise occur. Close monitoring and restrictions on the use of bottom-disturbing equipment would be needed to avoid or minimize those impacts.

Conclusion

There is a very low probability of a spill from the well sites occurring and contacting wetland environments due to the proximity to shore, absence of nearshore pipeline emplacement, and minimal vessel transport of product. Based on the low frequency of port visits the probability of impacts to coastal wetlands would be small. Should a spill make landfall and a cleanup proceed with approved procedures, impacts to wetlands would be minimal due to the weathered condition of the oil and the containment and cleanup techniques. Recovery periods longer than 2 years would be very unlikely. Therefore, no significant, long-term impacts to the structure or vitality of wetlands would be expected to occur from accidental spills of oil and diesel fuel.

During routine operations, vessel traffic will produce an incremental, if any, increase in erosion rates, sediment resuspension, and turbidity, an adverse but not significant impact to coastal wetland since the ports used can be approached using armored approach channels.

3.2.1.2.3. Cumulative Analysis

This cumulative analysis considers the effects of impact-producing factors related to the proposed action, prior and future OCS sales, State oil and gas activities, other governmental and private projects and activities, and pertinent natural processes and events that may occur and adversely affect wetlands. Conversion of wetlands to agricultural, residential, recreational, and commercial uses has generally been the major cause of wetland loss. The loss of wetlands is projected to continue in the Gulf Coast States. Deltaic Louisiana will continue to experience the greatest losses; wetland loss is also expected to continue in coastal Texas, Mississippi, Alabama, and Florida, but at slower rates. Approximately 2.1-2.4 percent of coastal wetland losses can be attributed to OCS oil and gas activities. The proposed action would represent a fraction of a percent contribution to these impacts.

Cumulative impacts on wetlands include the sources identified in Chapter 4.4.3 of the Multisale EIS (USDOI, MMS, 2007) and are hereby incorporated by reference into this PEA. Because 90 percent of coastal Louisiana is <1 m (3.3 ft) above sea level, subsidence and transgression of the sea can cause significant wetland loss or conversion into different environments. Estimates for wetland loss or conversion vary but most reported rates are close to 25 mi^2 (65 km^2) per year. A recent estimate predicted that about 640,000 ac (258,999 ha) of existing wetlands will be submerged in less than 50 years (Louisiana Coastal Wetlands Conservation and Restoration Task Force, 1993). There is increasing new evidence of the importance of the effect of sea-level rise (or marsh subsidence) as it relates to the loss of marsh or changes in marsh types and plant diversity (Spalding and Hester, 2007). This study shows that the very structure of coastal wetlands will likely be altered by sea-level rise, as community shifts will be governed by the responses of individual species to new environmental conditions. The effects of pipelines, canal dredging, navigation activities, and oil spills on wetlands are described in Chapters 4.2.1.1.3.2, 4.2.2.1.3.2, and 4.4.3.2 of the Multisale EIS. Subsidence of wetlands is discussed in more detail in Chapter 4.1.3.3.1 of the Multisale EIS (USDOI, MMS, 2007).

The continued increasing U.S. demand for petroleum combined with decreased domestic production will increase the need for imports, thereby increasing the tanker traffic and the need for more onshore production facilities. Consequently, it is the increases in oil imports in the form of increased tanker transits into GOM refinery ports and terminals that will drive the cumulative increase for the risk of oil spills. Impacts from State onshore oil and gas activities are expected to occur as a result of dredging for new canals, maintenance and usage of existing rig access canals and drill slips, and preparation of new well sites. Both of these activities (increased tanker traffic and State onshore oil and gas activities) may impact wetlands either through vessel-generated erosion or by requiring the expansion of production facilities into the wetlands.

Insignificant adverse impacts upon wetlands from maintenance dredging are expected because the large majority of the material would be disposed upon existing disposal areas. Alternative, dredged material disposal methods can be used to enhance and create coastal wetlands. Depending upon the regions and soils through which they were dredged, secondary adverse impacts of canals may be more locally significant than direct impacts. Additional wetland losses generated by the secondary impacts of saltwater intrusion, flank subsidence, freshwater-reservoir reduction, and deeper tidal penetration have not been calculated because of a lack of quantitative documentation; MMS has initiated a project to document and develop data concerning such losses.

Wetlands will continue to be impacted by natural events such as hurricanes, subsidence, saltwater intrusion, and sea-level rise. There is increasing new evidence of the importance of the effect of sea-level rise (or marsh subsidence) as it relates to the loss of marsh or changes in marsh types and plant diversity (Spalding and Hester, 2007). This study shows that the very structure of coastal wetlands will likely be altered by sea-level rise, as community shifts will be governed by the responses of individual species to new environmental conditions. In addition, the State of Louisiana has made provisions for wetlands protection and restoration part of the State's plan for hurricane protection. As climatic patterns vary, drought conditions may induce a need for additional reservoir storage and, as a result, alter the freshwater input into the coastal wetlands. Based of the reduction in freshwater input, salinity modifications may alter wetland type and, in some cases, allow for increased salinity intrusion into fresh marshes. The Louisiana State legislature established the Coastal Protection and Restoration Authority and charged it with coordinating the efforts of local, State, and Federal agencies to achieve long-term and comprehensive coastal protection and restoration that integrates flood control and wetland restoration.

In summary, the effects to coastal wetlands from the primary impact-producing activities associated with the proposed action are expected to be low. Maintenance dredging of navigation channels and canals is expected to occur with minimal impacts; the proposed action is expected to contribute minimally to the need for this dredging. Alternative dredged material disposal methods can be used to enhance and create coastal wetlands. Vessel traffic associated with the proposed action is expected to contribute minimally to the erosion and widening of navigation channels and canals. Overall, impacts from these sources are expected to be low and could be further reduced through mitigation, such as horizontal directional (trench less) drilling techniques to avoid damages to these sensitive habitats. Secondary impacts to wetlands would be primarily from vessel traffic corridors and will continue, but the impact can range from minimal to moderate but not significant depending on whether offshore or inland ports are used. In addition, inland ports with armored access will be minimally affected by the vessel traffic.

3.2.1.3. Alabama, Choctawhatchee, St. Andrew, and Perdido Key Beach Mice

3.2.1.3.1. Description

Sixteen subspecies of field mouse (*Peromyscus polionotus*) are recognized along the Gulf Coast, eight of which are collectively known as beach mice. The Alabama, Choctawhatchee, St. Andrew, and Perdido Key beach mice are designated as protected species under the Endangered Species Act (ESA) because of the loss of coastal habitat (USDOI, MMS, 2007).

Beach mice are characterized in Chapter 3.2.5 of the Multisale EIS (USDOI, MMS, 2007) and are hereby incorporated by reference into this PEA. A summary of the incorporated material follows.

Beach mice are restricted to the coastal barrier sand dunes along the Gulf Coast. Optimal overall beach mouse habitat is currently thought to be comprised of a heterogeneous mix of interconnected habitats including primary dunes, secondary dunes, scrub dunes, and interdunal areas. Beach mice dig burrows mainly in the primary, secondary, and interior scrub dunes where the vegetation provides suitable cover. Most beach mouse surveys conducted prior to the mid-1990's were in primary and secondary dunes because the investigators assumed that these habitats are the preferred habitat of beach mice.

Beach mice feed nocturnally in the dunes and remain in burrows during the day. Their diets vary seasonally but consist mainly of seeds, fruits, and insects (Ehrhart, 1978; Moyers, 1996). Changes in the availability of foods result in changes in diets between seasons and account for variability of seasonal diets between years.

Hurricanes are a natural environmental phenomenon affecting the Gulf Coast, and beach mice have evolved and persisted in coastal dune habitats since the Pleistocene. Hurricanes are part of a repeated cycle of destruction, alteration, and recovery of dune habitat. The extensive coastal dune habitat that existed along the Gulf Coast before the fairly recent commercial and residential development allowed beach mice to survive even the most severe hurricane events to repopulate dune habitat as it recovered. Beach mice are affected by the passage of hurricanes along the northwest Florida and Alabama Gulf Coast. Since records on hurricane intensity began in 1885, a total of 32 hurricanes have struck northwest Florida within the historic ranges of the four Gulf Coast beach mouse subspecies (Williams and Duedall, 1997; Doering et al., 1994; Neumann et al., 1993). In addition, 22 hurricanes have made landfall along the coast of Alabama from 1851 to 2004 (USDOC, NOAA, National Hurricane Center, 2006).

Beach mice have existed in an environment subject to recurring hurricanes, but tropical storms and hurricanes are now considered to be a primary factor in the beach mouse's decline. It is only within the last 20-30 years that the combination of habitat loss due to beachfront development, isolation of remaining beach mouse habitat blocks and populations, and destruction of remaining habitat by hurricanes have increased the threat of extinction of several subspecies of beach mice.

3.2.1.3.2. Impact Analysis

The major impact-producing factors associated with the proposed action that may affect beach mice include (1) oil spills, (2) spill-response activities, and (3) beach trash and debris from OCS activity. Chapters 4.2.2.1.7 and 4.4.7 of the Multisale EIS (USDOI, MMS, 2007) contain a discussion of impacts from OCS activity and are hereby incorporated by reference into this PEA. The incorporated materials are summarized below.

Direct contact with spilled oil that has washed ashore can cause skin and eye irritation, asphyxiation from the inhalation of fumes, oil ingestion, and reduction or contamination of food sources. Regardless of the potential for persistence of oil in beach mouse habitat, a slick cannot wash over the fore dunes unless carried by a heavy storm swell. High seas would be necessary to cause a spill slick to landfall and affect mice or their habitat. The erosion associated with high seas during storms is likely to do more damage to beach mouse habitat than oiling.

Vehicular traffic and activity associated with oil-spill cleanup can trample or bury nests and burrows or cause displacement from preferred habitat. Trash and debris may be mistakenly consumed by beach mice or it may ensnare them; however, contact between mice and trash originating from the proposed development activities in Green Canyon is very unlikely. The impacts on beach mice from oil spills and cleanup activities are discussed in Chapter 4.4.7 of the Multisale EIS (USDOI, MMS, 2007) and are hereby incorporated by reference into this PEA. Oil spills or cleanup activity and incidental trash related to the proposed activity are not expected to significantly impact beach mice.

Conclusion

Impacts from the proposed development activities in the Green Canyon area on the Alabama, Choctawhatchee, St. Andrew, and Perdido Key beach mice are unlikely. Impacts may result from the consumption of beach trash and debris. The proposed activities would deposit only a small portion of the total debris that would reach the habitat. Efforts undertaken for the removal of marine debris may temporarily scare away beach mice, destroy their food resources, or collapse the tops of their burrows.

Given the low probability of a large (≥1,000 bbl) oil spill occurring, direct impacts of spills on beach mice from the proposed action are highly unlikely. Oil-spill response and cleanup activities could have significant impact on the beach mice and their habitat if not properly regulated.

3.2.1.3.3. Cumulative Analysis

Cumulative activities have a potential to harm or reduce the numbers of Alabama, Choctawhatchee, St. Andrew, and Perdido Key beach mice. Those activities include oil spills, alteration and reduction of habitat, predation and competition, and consumption of beach trash and debris. Spills from the Phoenix development activities, as well as oil spills stemming from service vessels, are not expected to contact beach mice or their habitats. Cumulative activities posing the greatest potential harm to beach mice are non-OCS activities (beach development and coastal spills) and natural catastrophes (hurricanes), which, in combination, could potentially deplete some beach mice populations to unsustainable levels. The expected incremental contribution of the proposed development activities to the cumulative impacts is negligible.

3.2.2. Sensitive Offshore Resources

Sensitive offshore environments in the Central Gulf are characterized in Chapters 3.2.2, 3.2.3, 3.2.4, 3.2.6, 3.2.7, and 3.2.8 of the Multisale EIS (USDOI, MMS, 2007) and are hereby incorporated by reference into this PEA. Summaries of these resources follow and include (1) deepwater benthic communities, (2) marine mammals, (3) sea turtles, (4) essential fish habitat and fish resources, (5) Gulf sturgeon, and (6) coastal and marine birds.

The impact-producing factors associated with the proposed Phoenix Project in Green Canyon Blocks 236 and 237 that could affect deepwater benthic communities, marine mammals, sea turtles, essential fish habitat and fish resources, Gulf sturgeon, and coastal and marine birds include (1) physical contact with anchors, mooring lines, and other engineered structures; (2) noise in the air and sea; (3) collisions with vessels; (4) lights in the remote offshore environment; (4) spilled oil and response activities; (5) effluent discharges; and (6) solid trash and debris. Discussions of the impacts from OCS activity on deepwater benthic communities, marine mammals, sea turtles, essential fish habitat and fish resources, Gulf sturgeon, and coastal and marine birds can be found in Chapters 4.2.1.1.4 through 4.2.1.1.8, 4.2.2.1.4 through 4.2.2.1.6, 4.2.2.1.8 through 4.2.2.1.10, and 4.4.10 of the Multisale EIS (USDOI, MMS, 2007) and are hereby incorporated by reference into this PEA.

Of these potential impact-producing factors, oil spills represent a high consequence and low-probability accidental event. No blowouts are projected as a result of development drilling, well completions, workovers, or hydrocarbon production associated with the Phoenix Project based on historical trends in the GOM (**Table B-1**). Spills that occur from development and production activity for the Phoenix Project would be few (if any), volumetrically small, and be located near project activities in Green Canyon Blocks 236 and 237.

Table B-4 indicates Gulfwide oil-spill occurrence rates. The statistics show that there have been numerous spills of >1 but <50 bbl but very few spills ≥1,000 bbl for all OCS operations per billion barrels of oil handled. A blowout is the only accident category that could yield a spill ≥1,000 bbl over the 5-year life cycle of Phoenix field production. The probability of a blowout is small, less than 1 in 100,000, and the combined probability of a spill ≥1,000 bbl making landfall in Louisiana or adjacent states would be extremely small (<0.5%).

Spills occurring in the deepwater environment of Grid 9 would not be large enough to enable them to persist long enough in the marine environment before weathering processes significantly degrade the spill before it makes landfalls. The transport time would allow a slick to weather, dissolve, and disperse while still in the marine environment. If a spill occurs at sea, mechanical cleanup is assumed to collect up to 10 percent of spilled oil and approximately 30 percent is assumed to be chemically dispersed, further reducing the overall probability and severity of spills that may move inshore. Because the landfall of spilled oil, diesel fuel, drilling fluids, or chemicals is highly unlikely, the potential impacts from spill landfall, i.e., response and cleanup activities on coastal barrier beaches and associated dunes and wetlands, are not expected to be incurred.

Cumulative impacts on sensitive offshore resources include those that affect animals living in and on the sea bottom and in the water column, as well as those animals that require nearshore or coastal resources for part of their lifecycle. The cumulative impacts on these resources are discussed below.

3.2.2.1. Deepwater Benthic Communities

3.2.2.1.1. Nonchemosynthetic Communities

3.2.2.1.1.1. Description

The description of the biology, life history, and distribution of nonchemosynthetic deepwater benthic communities can be found in Chapter 3.2.2.2.2 of the Multisale EIS. The vast majority of the GOM has a soft, muddy bottom in which burrowing infauna are the most abundant invertebrates. The Green Canyon Blocks 236 and 237 area falls into this category, and proposed wells are at a water depth ranging from

1,630 to 2,335 m (5,346 to 7,724 ft). Using complete 3D seismic seabed amplitude anomaly coverage of the area, no new hard bottoms were discovered in Green Canyon Block 236. There are no known hard-bottom areas in Green Canyon Block 236, and an area of Green Canyon Block 237 with some potentially exposed hard bottom is well removed from impacting activities (see also **Chapter 3.2.2.1.2**, Chemosynthetic Communities).

As in all areas of the Gulf, a wide variety of organisms, ranging from single-celled bacteria to invertebrates and fish, inhabit soft-bottom habitat at almost every depth range in the Gulf of Mexico. These organisms can also include chemosynthetic animals, a remarkable assemblage of invertebrates found in association with hydrocarbon seeps that use a carbon source independent of photosynthesis and the sun-dependent photosynthetic food chain that supports most all other life on earth. This unique group is discussed in **Chapter 3.2.2.1.2**. Also, recent study results in Rowe and Kennicutt (2002) have indicated some unique areas of soft-bottom communities with substantially higher community biomass and carbon flux near the Mississippi River Delta.

The continental slope in the GOM extends from the edge of the continental shelf at about 200 m (656 ft) to a water depth of approximately 3,000 m (9,840 ft). Green Canyon Blocks 236 and 237 lie in the mid levels of the continental slope, which corresponds to the depth zone termed archibenthal, as characterized by Pequegnat (1983) and Gallaway et al. (1988).

The vast majority of the GOM seabed is comprised of soft sediments. Major groups of animals that live in this habitat include (1) bacteria and other microbenthos, (2) meiofauna (0.063-0.3 mm (0.00248-0.0118 in)), (3) macrofauna (>0.3 mm (0.0118)), and (4) megafauna (larger organisms such as crabs, sea pens, sea cucumbers, crinoids, and bottom-dwelling (demersal) fish). All of these groups are represented throughout the entire Gulf—from the continental shelf to the deepest abyssal depths (about 3,850 m or 12,630 ft). Basic descriptions of typical soft-bottom fauna (bacteria, meiofauna, macrofauna, and megafauna) are addressed in Chapter 3.2.2.2 of the Multisale EIS. Representatives from all of these groups would be expected in the Phoenix Green Canyon Blocks 236 and 237 area. A great number of publications have been derived from two major MMS-funded deep Gulf studies; Rowe and Kennicutt (2002) and Gallaway et al. (1988). These two studies provide for extensive background information on deepwater GOM habitat and biological communities.

3.2.2.1.1.2. Impact Analysis

The potential impacts to nonchemosynthetic deepwater benthic communities expected to inhabit Green Canyon Blocks 236 and 237 are discussed below.

The impact-producing factors associated with exploration of the Phoenix Project in Green Canyon Blocks 236 and 237 that could affect nonchemosynthetic deepwater benthic communities include (1) drilling discharges, including primarily cuttings with adhering drilling muds, and (2) seafloor disturbance from possible blowouts during well drilling. The deepwater ecosystem in Green Canyon Blocks 236 and 237 can be characterized as vast expanses of soft-bottom faunas. The topography is sloped to the south, decreasing in depth around 700 m (2,297 ft) between the shallowest and deepest well sites.

The most important impact-producing factors on nonchemosynthetic deepwater benthic communities are physical disturbances of the seafloor caused by the deposition of drilling cuttings and associated drilling fluids. Significant accumulation thickness will be limited to a relatively close distance from the surface discharge point. A recent study looked at both exploratory and production facility drilling discharges in water depths of 1,000 m (3,280 ft) and reported detectable accumulations at distances as far as 1 km (0.6 mi) (CSA, 2006). Geophysically mapped thicknesses of cuttings accumulations at one site showed a rapid decrease of thickness with increasing distance from the well site. Accumulation thickness was less than 7.6 cm (3 in) within 240 m (787 ft) of the well site. The maximum bottom area disturbed in any way is estimated to be no larger than 315 ha (778 ac), assuming the worst case of muds and cuttings discharges reaching distances of 1,000 m (3,280 ft) from the well site in every direction (CSA, 2006). Realistically, splays of discharges only move to limited directions depending on prevailing currents; a good estimate would be 1/3 of the radius of a circle or 105 ha out to 1,000 m (260 ac out to 3,280 ft). This would not result in a significant impact on the nonchemosynthetic benthic communities because the duration and areal extent of the proposed activities would be limited, and recolonization of benthic communities is facilitated from nearby surrounding areas.

A DP semisubmersible platform will be used to drill new wells; therefore, there will be no new impact from anchoring. The DP semisubmersible drilling rig will be installed near the previous position of the Typhoon TLP that was destroyed by Hurricane Rita in September 2005. Anchor impacts from the buoy installation (for use with the FPU) will extend farther from this location but remain in areas of soft mud-bottom habitat.

A blowout at the seafloor could create a crater on the sea bottom and resuspend and disperse large quantities of bottom sediments within a 300-m (984-ft) radius of the blowout site, burying both infaunal (live in the sediment) and epifaunal (live on sediment) organisms and interfering with sessile invertebrates that rely on filter-feeding organs. Impacts of rapid burial are discussed in Chapter 4.1.1 in the Multisale EIS. Similar to impacts from drill cuttings, impacts from a blowout would be limited because the duration and areal extent would be limited, and recolonization of communities is facilitated from nearby surrounding areas.

Conclusion

The proposed Phoenix Project is expected to have negligible impacts on the ecological function, biological productivity, or distribution of soft-bottom, nonchemosynthetic benthic communities. Bottom disturbances from the discharge of drilling cuttings and associated drilling muds will not be of a sufficient size or duration to adversely affect these benthic community types to any significant or permanent degree. Minor and temporary impacts, such as interference with filter-feeding structures, could occur over areas inside an envelope estimated to be no more than about 105 ha out to 1,000 m (260 ac out to 3,280 ft). Routine discharges are not expected to adversely impact these community types because of the water depths in Green Canyon Blocks 236 and 237. Anchor impacts from the installation of a buoy will be minor and similar to the previously installed Typhoon TLP near the same site. Bottom disturbance from a blowout during the drilling of the wells is not likely based on the historical record of blowout events in the Gulf. Recruitment of new organisms would take place from nearby areas, and organisms from undisturbed areas are free to migrate into disrupted areas after the disturbance ceases.

3.2.2.1.1.3. Cumulative Analysis

Cumulative impacts on nonchemosynthetic deepwater benthic communities include crushing and physical disturbance of the sea bottom from drilling discharges and emplacement of other drilling rigs, production platforms, and subsea production infrastructure. The water depth in the Green Canyon Blocks 236 and 237 area ranges from 1,630 to 2,335 m (5,346 to 7,724 ft). These depths are too deep for anchoring by service vessels, which will use a mooring buoy system. There are no non-OCS activities (e.g., commercial bottom trawling) that could cause sea-bottom disturbances. The cumulative impacts on nonchemosynthetic benthic communities are expected to cause little damage to the ecological function or biological productivity of the expected typical communities existing on sand/silt/clay bottoms of the deep Green Canyon Blocks 236 and 237 area of the GOM. Large motile animals would tend to move, and recolonization from populations from neighboring substrates would be expected in any areas impacted by any form of burial.

3.2.2.1.2. Chemosynthetic Communities

3.2.2.1.2.1. Description

The description of the chemosynthetic deepwater benthic communities in the GOM can be found in Chapter 3.2.2.2.1 of the Multisale EIS (USDOI, MMS, 2007). The following information is a summary of the description hereby incorporated by reference from the Multisale EIS.

Chemosynthetic communities are defined as persistent, largely sessile assemblages of marine organisms dependent upon symbiotic chemosynthetic bacteria as their primary food source (MacDonald, 1992). Chemosynthetic clams, mussels, and tube worms are similar to (but not identical with) the hydrothermal vent communities of the eastern Pacific (Corliss et al., 1979). Bacteria live within specialized cells in these invertebrate organisms and are supplied with oxygen and chemosynthetic compounds by the host via specialized blood chemistry (Fisher, 1990). The host, in turn, lives off the organic products subsequently released by the chemosynthetic bacteria and may even feed on the bacteria themselves. Additional information on the biology, life history and distribution of chemosynthetic deepwater benthic communities can be found in Chapter 3.2.2.2 of the Multisale EIS (USDOI, MMS, 2007).

Chemosynthetic communities in the CPA have been reported to occur at water depths between 290 and 2,743 m (951 and 9,000 ft) (USDOI, MMS, 2007). The total number of chemosynthetic communities in the Gulf is now known to exceed 60. A recent MMS study, *Investigations of Chemosynthetic Communities on the Lower Continental Slope of the Gulf of Mexico* (Brooks et al., in press), has performed exploration surveys specifically targeting water depths below 1,000 m (3,280 ft). This project confirmed the presence of 12 additional chemosynthetic communities not previously know in these water depths. What was initially thought to be relatively rare occurrences of chemosynthetic communities is now known to be far more common and regularly associated with primary geophysical signatures of the seabed including faulting with conduits for hydrocarbons to the surface from deeper depths and precipitation of carbonate deposits on the sea floor. Anomalies of seismic survey acoustic amplitudes on the seabed is one major feature related to most all known chemosynthetic communities and these kinds of features are now relatively well mapped throughout the entire northern Gulf of Mexico. The total number of features on the northern Gulf slope that have probable associated communities now number in the thousands.

A review for the potential occurrence of chemosynthetic communities associated with Green Canyon Blocks 236 and 237 for the proposed Phoenix Project was performed for this PEA. Green Canyon Blocks 236 and 237 lie in a region with numerous areas of gas expulsion and areas of high probability for the presence of chemosynthetic communities. There is one major feature in Green Canyon Block 237 to the northwest of one well and the FPU location that is a high-probability area for chemosynthetic communities. Other high-probability areas occur to the northwest in Green Canyon Block 235, to the northeast in Green Canyon Block 193, to the southwest in Green Canyon Block 324, and to the southeast in Green Canyon Block 283. All but the feature in Green Canyon Block 237 lie several miles distant from the Phoenix activities.

3.2.2.1.2.2. Impact Analysis

A detailed impact analysis of the routine, accidental, and cumulative impacts of the proposed exploration activities on chemosynthetic communities can be found in Chapters 4.2.1.1.4.2.1, 4.2.2.1.4.2.1, 4.4.4.2.1, and 4.5.4.1 of the Multisale EIS (USDOI, MMS, 2007). The following information is a summary of the impact analysis incorporated by reference from the Multisale EIS.

The NTL 2000-G20, "Deepwater Chemosynthetic Communities," makes mandatory the search for and avoidance of dense chemosynthetic communities (such as Bush Hill-type communities) or areas that have a high potential for supporting these community types, as interpreted from geophysical records. The NTL is exercised on all applicable leases and is not an optional protective measure. The closest feature with the potential to support chemosynthetic communities will be avoided by at least 1,550 ft (472 m) by both anchors and drilling discharges. There are no anticipated impacts to any chemosynthetic communities as a result of the Phoenix Project.

Conclusion

The proposed Phoenix Project is not expected to impact either known or probable areas of high-density chemosynthetic communities. The nearest potential for any chemosynthetic community in proximity to Green Canyon Blocks 236 and 237 is approximately 1,500 ft (472 m) to the east of anchor leg #1 for the FPU in Green Canyon Block 237. No high-density chemosynthetic community components occur in the vicinity of the proposed drilling at any of the proposed six well sites in Green Canyon Blocks 236 and 237.

3.2.2.1.2.3. Cumulative Analysis

Cumulative impacts on chemosynthetic communities include the sources identified in Chapter 3.2.2.2 of the Multisale EIS (USDOI, MMS, 2007). No additional impacts to chemosynthetic communities from either OCS or non-OCS-related activities would be expected. Normal fishing practices should not disturb the bottom in these areas. Bottom-disturbing activities such as trawling and boat anchoring are virtually nonexistent at water depths >400 m (1,312 ft). In addition, there are no chemosynthetic communities expected in any of the impacted areas. Cumulative impacts from activity in Green Canyon Blocks 236 and 237 are not expected. No impacts from non-OCS-related activities would be expected.

3.2.2.2. *Marine Mammals*

3.2.2.2.1. Description

Twenty-eight cetaceans (whales and dolphins) and one sirenian (manatee) species have confirmed occurrences in the northern GOM (Davis and Fargion, 1996). Detailed information on each listed marine mammal species can be found in Chapter 3.2.3 of the Multisale EIS (USDOI, MMS, 2007) and is hereby incorporated by reference into this PEA, a brief summary follows. Cetaceans are divided into two major suborders: Mysticeti (baleen whales) and Odontoceti (toothed whales and dolphins). Of the six baleen whale species occurring in the Gulf, four are listed as endangered or threatened (Table 3-4 of the Multisale EIS (USDOI, MMS, 2007)). Of the 21 toothed whale species occurring in the Gulf, only the sperm whale is listed as endangered. The only member of the Order Sirenia found in the Gulf is the endangered West Indian manatee. The manatee has been reported in Louisiana coastal waters, but the coastal waters of Peninsular Florida and the Florida Panhandle are the manatee's normal habitat.

The MMS has been conducting scientific research of marine mammals in the GOM since 1991, including GulfCet I and II and the Sperm Whale Acoustic Monitoring Program (SWAMP). The most recent study, Sperm Whale Seismic Study (SWSS), completed four years of field work in 2005. This multi-faceted program involved numerous partners and researchers. Yearly reports have been published, and a synthesis report of the SWSS study will be published in 2008 (Jochens et al., 2008). These studies have shown that the GOM has a diverse and abundant marine mammal community, including a genetically-distinct resident population of the endangered sperm whale.

3.2.2.2.2. Impact Analysis

The impact-producing factors associated with exploration of the Phoenix Project that could affect marine mammals include (1) noise from vessel traffic, air traffic, and exploration activities; (2) degradation of water quality from oil spills or other material spills; (3) collision potential with service vessels; (4) spill-response activities; and (5) trash and debris from structures and service vessels. These impact-producing factors are the same for nonthreatened and nonendangered marine mammal species as well as those listed under the ESA. Chapters 4.2.1.1.5 and 4.2.2.1.5 of the Multisale EIS (USDOI, MMS, 2007) contain a discussion of impacts from OCS activity and are hereby incorporated by reference into this PEA.

Operations

The noise and shadow from helicopter overflights, take-offs, and landings can cause a startle response and can interrupt whales and dolphins while resting, feeding, breeding, or migrating (Richardson et al., 1995). Frequent overflights could have long-term consequences if they repeatedly or consistently disrupt important life functions such as feeding and breeding.

The proposed action is expected to have three helicopter roundtrips per week, as needed. These occurrences would be temporary and pass within seconds. As more industry development projects occur in the area, helicopter activity is expected to increase. However, marine mammals are not expected to be adversely affected by routine helicopter traffic operating at prescribed altitudes.

Many types of plastic materials end up as solid waste during drilling and production operations. Some of this material is accidentally lost overboard where whales and dolphins can consume or become ensnared in it. The result of plastic ingestion is certainly deleterious and could be lethal. The probability of a marine mammal encountering trash that appears edible is probably very low. The disposal of solid wastes offshore takes place in covered bins that are warehoused in a secure area on the DP semisubmersible, and the bins are returned to shore by service vessels for disposal.

Service vessels present a collision hazard to marine mammals. The Phoenix Project is expected to require two supply-vessel and crew-vessel roundtrips per week. The consequence of a vessel collision and a marine mammal is likely to be lethal, but the probability of a collision taking place is low with the current mitigations in place.

Accidental Events

Spills that occur from Phoenix Project would be few (if any) if they did occur. Oil spills and spill-response activities have the potential to adversely affect whales and dolphins by causing soft tissue irritation, fouling of baleen plates, respiratory stress from inhalation of toxic fumes, food reduction or contamination, direct ingestion of oil and/or tar, and temporary displacement from preferred habitats or migration routes. Some short-term (months) effects of oil may be as follows: (1) changes in cetacean distribution associated with avoidance of aromatic hydrocarbons and surface oil; (2) changes in prey distribution and human disturbance; (3) increased mortality rates from ingestion or inhalation of oil; (4) increased petroleum compounds in tissues; and (5) impaired health (e.g., immunosuppression) (Harvey and Dahlheim, 1994). Potential mechanisms for long-term injury include (1) initial sublethal exposure to oil causing pathological damage; (2) continued exposure to hydrocarbons persisting in the environment, either directly or through ingestion of contaminated prey; and (3) altered availability of prey as a result of the spill (Ballachey et al., 1994). Chronic effects may include (1) change in distribution and abundance because of reduced prey resources or increased mortality rates, (2) change in age structure in the breeding stock because certain year-classes were impacted more by an oil spill, (3) decreased reproductive success, and (4) increased rate of disease or neurological problems from exposure to oil (Harvey and Dahlheim, 1994).

Clearly, the vitality or productivity of some marine mammals can suffer long-term impacts from oil spills, but the evidence for cetaceans being among this affected population has not been convincingly established. There is, however, substantial circumstantial evidence based on effects documented in other marine mammals that harmful effects from contact between spilled oil and individual whales or dolphins can be reasonably expected. Contact between marine mammals and spilled oil is unlikely, and the duration of this contact with mobile animals in the open ocean is expected to be very brief. Effects on marine mammal populations are expected to be insignificant.

Conclusion

The proposed Phoenix Project is expected to have little impact on the vitality of any marine mammal species or productivity of any population endemic to the northern GOM. No deaths would be expected from direct exposure to spilled oil or to chronic long-term effects caused by contact with spilled oil. Although interaction between marine mammals and a weathered oil spill is possible, sublethal effects would be the likely result. Collisions between service vessels and marine mammals would be extremely rare, but they could be lethal or crippling if realized. The MMS's regulations and NTL's are designed to reduce the possibility of collisions. There is no conclusive evidence as to whether or not anthropogenic noise in the water has caused displacements of marine mammal populations or is injurious to the vitality of individuals. Marine mammals could be injured or killed by eating indigestible debris or plastic items originating from the proposed development activities, but the likelihood of such an encounter is very small. Marine mammal populations are not expected to be adversely impacted by routine discharges due to current regulations and guidelines, and rapid dilution.

3.2.2.2.3. Cumulative Analysis

Cumulative impacts on marine mammals include (1) water quality degradation from oil, fuel, and material spills, high nutrient loads, high turbidity, high BOD, urban runoff, industrial discharges, pathogens, and upriver contaminants; (2) noise in the water from infrastructure, vessels, and facility removal; (3) vessel traffic and collision hazard; (4) seismic surveying; and (5) trash and debris. Non-OCS activity that contributes to cumulative impacts includes the same impact-producing factors from OCS activity, but which arise from other industrial, commercial, or recreational activity. Marine mammal deaths attributable to non-OCS activity, such as commercial fishing, would be much greater than any caused by OCS activity.

Of these effects, the potential for collision between marine mammals and service vessels probably represents the greatest potential for adverse cumulative impacts on marine mammals over the 5-year exploration and production cycle. This judgment is made because collisions between large vessels and cetaceans, though rare events, typically results in crippling injuries or death. Marine mammals could be injured or killed from ensnarement in or consumption of marine debris, particularly plastic items, lost from OCS structures and service vessels. Few deaths would be expected from chance collisions between marine mammals and OCS service vessels, ingestion of debris such as plastic material, and pathogens.

Oil spills and associated slicks of any size are infrequent events, but if they do occur they have a very small potential to contact marine mammals. Sublethal effects could occur with exposure of marine mammals to a weathered oil slick. Disturbance (noise from vessel traffic and drilling operations, etc.)

and/or exposure to platform discharges may cause sublethal effects, may stress animals and weaken their immune systems, and may make them more vulnerable to parasites and diseases.

The net result of any disturbance would be dependent upon the size and percentage of the population affected, ecological importance of the disturbed area, environmental and biological parameters that influence an animal's sensitivity to disturbance and stress, and the accommodation time in response to prolonged disturbance (Geraci and St. Aubin, 1980).

3.2.2.3. Sea Turtles

3.2.2.3.1. Description

Five species of sea turtles are found in the waters of the GOM: green, leatherback, hawksbill, Kemp's ridley, and loggerhead. All are protected under the ESA, and all except the loggerhead turtle (threatened) are listed as endangered. Detailed information on each listed sea turtles species can be found in Chapter 3.2.4 of the Multisale EIS (USDOI, MMS, 2007) and is hereby incorporated by reference into this PEA; a brief summary follows. Sea turtles are long-lived, slow-reproducing animals that spend nearly all of their lives in the water. Females must emerge periodically from the ocean to nest on beaches. It is generally believed that all sea turtle species spend their first few years in pelagic waters, occurring in driftlines and convergence zones (in *Sargassum* rafts) where they find refuge and food in items that accumulate in surface circulation features (Carr and Caldwell, 1956; Carr, 1987). Genetic analysis of sea turtles has revealed in recent years that discrete, non-interbreeding stocks of sea turtles make up "worldwide extensive ranges" of the various species.

Adult turtles are apparently less abundant in the deeper waters of the Gulf than they are in waters less than 27-50 m (80-160 ft) deep (NRC, 1990) and more abundant in the northeastern Gulf than in the northwestern Gulf (Thompson, 1988). Sea turtle abundance appears to increase dramatically east of Mobile Bay (Davis et al., 2000). Factors such as water depth and turbidity, bottom sediment type, salinity, and prey availability may account for this. In the offshore Gulf, sea turtle distribution has been linked to zones of convergence.

Information on each turtle species can be found in Chapter 3.2.4 and Table 3-5 of the Multisale EIS (USDOI, MMS, 2007) and is hereby incorporated by reference into this PEA.

3.2.2.3.2. Impact Analysis

The impact-producing factors associated with exploration of the Phoenix Project that could affect loggerhead, Kemp's ridley, hawksbill, green, and leatherback turtles, (all listed as endangered or threatened species) include (1) noise from helicopter, platform, and vessel traffic; (2) possible collisions with service vessels; (3) brightly-lit structures; (4) project-related trash and debris; (5) oil spills and spill-response activities; and (6) water-quality degradation from platform effluents. Chapters 4.2.1.1.6 and 4.2.2.1.6 of the Multisale EIS (USDOI, MMS, 2007) contain a discussion of impacts from OCS activity and are hereby incorporated by reference into this PEA.

Operations

The noise from helicopter operation can elicit a startle response and can interrupt sea turtles while resting, feeding, breeding, or migrating. The proposed action is expected to have three helicopter roundtrips per week, as needed. These occurrences would be temporary and pass within seconds. There are no published systematic studies about the reactions of sea turtles to aircraft overflights, and anecdotal reports are scarce. Sea turtles spend more than 70 percent of their time underwater, but it is assumed that sea turtles can hear helicopter noise at or near the surface and that unexpected noise may cause animals to alter their activity (Advanced Research Projects Agency, 1995). There is evidence suggesting that turtles may be receptive to low-frequency sounds, which is the level where most industrial noise energy is concentrated. Atmospheric noise inputs, however, are negligible relative to other sources of noise that are propagated in water (e.g., platform or drill rig operations and vessel traffic). It is unlikely that sea turtles would be adversely affected by routine helicopter traffic operating at prescribed altitudes.

Brightly-lit, offshore drilling rigs and platforms present a potential distraction to hatchlings (Owens, 1983). Hatchlings are known to be attracted to light (Raymond, 1984; Witherington and Martin, 1996; Witherington, 1997) and could be expected to orient toward lighted offshore facilities (Chan and Liew,

1988). If this occurs, hatchling predation would increase dramatically since large birds and predacious fish also congregate around the platforms (Owens, 1983; Witherington and Martin, 1996). The very short duration of the light attraction for hatchlings, however, would indicate that this is a risk only for facilities very close to nesting beaches.

Many types of materials, including plastic wrapping materials, end up as solid waste during exploration operations. Some of this material could be accidentally lost overboard where sea turtles can consume it. The result of ingesting materials lost overboard could be lethal. Leatherback turtles are known to mistake plastics for jellyfish and may be more vulnerable to gastrointestinal blockage than other sea turtle species. The probability of a sea turtle encountering trash that appears edible is probably very low. Sea turtles could also become entangled or suffer crippling injuries from debris that is lost by service vessels. Disposal of solid wastes offshore takes place in covered bins that are warehoused in a secure area on the platform, whereupon the bins are returned to shore for landfill disposal by a service vessel for landfill disposal.

Service vessels present a collision hazard to sea turtles. The Phoenix Project is expected to require two supply-vessel and crew-vessel roundtrips per week. As additional projects are pursued by industry in the area, increased ship traffic levels could increase the probability of collisions between ships and sea turtles, resulting in injury or death to some animals.

Accidental Events

Spills that occur from the Phoenix Project activities would be few (if any) if they did occur. When an oil spill occurs, the severity of effects and the extent of damage to sea turtles are affected by (1) geographic location, (2) hydrocarbon type, (3) duration of contact, (4) weathering state of a slick, (5) impact area, (6) oceanographic and meteorological conditions, (7) season, and (8) growth stage of the animal (NRC, 1985). All sea turtle species and life stages are vulnerable to the harmful effects of oil through direct contact or by fouling of their habitats and food.

No deaths would be expected from direct exposure to spilled oil or to chronic long-term effects. Several potential mechanisms for long-term impacts may be (1) sublethal initial exposure to oil, causing pathological damage and weakening of body systems or inhibiting reproductive success; (2) chronic exposure to residual hydrocarbons persisting in the environment or through ingestion of contaminated prey; and (3) altered prey availability as a result of the spill. Turtles may be temporarily displaced from areas impacted by spills. Because sea turtle habitat in the Gulf includes coastal and oceanic waters, as well as numerous beaches in the region, sea turtles could be impacted by accidental spills from vessels supporting the proposed action that are in transit near these environments. Although there is documentation of the harmful effects of acute exposure to spilled oil, the effects of chronic exposure are less certain and are largely inferred. An interaction between sea turtles at sea and spilled oil are unlikely to be realized. Contact between sea turtles and spilled oil is very unlikely, and the duration of this contact with mobile animals in the open ocean would be very brief. Adverse effects on sea turtle populations are expected to be insignificant.

Oil-spill-response activities, such as beach sand removal, can adversely affect sea turtles. Vehicular and vessel traffic during spill-response actions in sensitive habitats during nesting season can occur. Harm to sea turtles is expected to be minimal because of the very low probability of contact between oil and these areas and protective spill remediation procedures. Increased human presence in nesting habitats could alter behavior of turtles, reduce their distribution, or cause them to move to less favorable areas, making them more vulnerable to various physiologic and toxic effects.

Conclusion

The proposed Phoenix Project is expected to have little impact on the vitality of any sea turtle species or productivity of any population endemic to the northern GOM. A sublethal impact to sea turtle individuals exposed to a weathered oil slick is the most likely result. There is no conclusive evidence whether or not anthropogenic noise in the water has caused displacements of sea turtle populations or is injurious to the vitality of individuals. Collisions between service vessels and sea turtles would be rare, but they could be lethal if realized. Sea turtles could be injured or killed by eating indigestible debris or plastic items originating from Phoenix activities, but the likelihood of such an encounter is very small.

3.2.2.3.3. Cumulative Analysis

Cumulative impacts on sea turtles and their habitats include (1) water quality degradation from oil, fuel, and other chemical spills, high nutrient loads, high turbidity, urban runoff, industrial discharges, pathogens, and upriver contaminants; (2) habitat loss or degradation; (3) infrastructure and vessel noise, lighting, and removal; (4) vessel traffic and collision hazard; (5) trash and debris; and (6) natural phenomena such as sea-level rise, subsidence, and storms and hurricanes. Non-OCS activity that contributes to cumulative impacts include commercial and recreational fishing that kill or injure turtles by accident, beach lighting, and entrainment in power plant intakes. The cumulative impacts from the major impact-producing factors on sea turtles would be dominantly sublethal, primarily behavioral changes, temporary disturbances, or displacement of localized groups, and rarely lethal. Turtle deaths attributable to non-OCS activity are expected to be greater than any caused by OCS activity.

Of these effects, dislocation from preferred beach-nesting habitats or destruction of these habitats probably represents the greatest potential for adverse cumulative impacts on sea turtles over the 5-year exploration and production cycle. The Phoenix Project is far from shoreline nesting habitat, and any bright lighting on the site should have no effect on sea turtle hatchlings.

Deaths due to explosive structure-removal operations should not take place or should be extremely rare with the explosive removal mitigations required by MMS. Underwater noise from platforms or service boats may disrupt normal activities and may cause physiological stress, causing turtles to become more susceptible to disease or predation. Collision hazards from service vessels would be expected to decrease because of mitigations put into place by MMS.

There are prohibitions on discarding trash or debris from project activity at sea. Sea turtles could be injured or killed from ensnarement in or consumption of marine debris, particularly plastic items, lost from OCS structures and service vessels.

Oil spills, chemical dispersants, and spill-response activities on sensitive nesting coastlines are potential hazards that may adversely affect sea turtles or the reproductive success of populations. Contact with and consumption of oil and oil-contaminated prey may seriously affect sea turtles. Large spills are extremely rare events, and for this reason no contact or interaction is expected between turtles and freshly spilled oil. Incidental contact with degraded or weathered oil may be expected between turtles that inhabit or transit through the Phoenix Project area. The effects from contact with spilled oil in a weathered slick would be sublethal behavioral changes.

The incremental contribution of the proposed Phoenix Project to the cumulative impacts would be negligible. The effects of the most likely impacts, such as the physical presence and operation of the DP semisubmersible drilling rig, or noise from the drilling rig, helicopters, and service-vessel traffic, would only be expected to modify the behavior of turtles that come into contact with these project facilities.

3.2.2.4. *Essential Fish Habitat and Fish Resources*

3.2.2.4.1. Description

The description of essential fish habitat (EFH) and fish resources in this deep Gulf of Mexico region can be found in Chapter 3.2.8 of the Multisale EIS (USDOI, MMS, 2007). The following information is a brief summary of the description that is hereby incorporated by reference from the Multisale EIS.

Healthy fish resources and fishery stocks depend on EFH—waters and substrate necessary to fish for spawning, breeding, feeding, and growth to maturity. The most recent Generic Amendment to all fishery management plans (GMFMC, 2005) reduced the extent of EFH relative to the 1998 Generic Amendment by removing EFH description and identification from waters between 100 fathoms (183 m or 600 ft) and the seaward limit of the Exclusive Economic Zone (as deep as 3,200 m or 10,499 ft). However, the habitats most important to managed species (i.e., those shallower than 100 fathoms (183 m or 600 ft)) will still be designated as EFH, and so the great majority of benefits to the biological environment will remain.

The benthic fish populations of Green Canyon Blocks 236 and 237 are expected to be low in density and restricted to species that live at water depths below 500 m. No benthic species in these blocks are included in any fishery management plan and description of EFH. Discussion of other ecological groups of fishes, including oceanic pelagics and mesopelagics, can be found in Chapter 3.2.8.2 of the Multisale EIS (USDOI, MMS, 2007). The EFH of Green Canyon Blocks 236 and 237 does retain EFH designation for some specific species, including many highly migratory species such as tunas, swordfish, and sailfish.

In consideration of existing mitigation measures, lease stipulations, and a submitted EFH Assessment document, MMS entered into a Programmatic Consultation agreement with NMFS on July 1, 1999, for petroleum development activities in the CPA and WPA. This agreement was extended into that portion of the EPA known as the Sale 181 Area. Most of the Sale 181 Area is now designated part of the CPA. The NMFS concluded EFH consultation with the MMS on the Multisale EIS (USDOI, MMS, 2007) through a letter dated December 21, 2006, and concurred with all activities described, with no additional conservation recommendations beyond those followed routinely by MMS. This consultation also includes Green Canyon Blocks 236 and 237 as well as all of Grid 9.

It is understood that all previously accepted EFH Conservation Recommendations provided by NMFS in the past will be continued. There have been six additional EFH conservation recommendations provided by NMFS in addition to standard MMS policies (USDOI, MMS, 2007; Chapter 3.2.8.2). The MMS has accepted and adopted these six additional EFH conservation recommendations.

3.2.2.4.2. Impact Analysis

The impact-producing factors associated with the drilling of additional wells in the Phoenix Project in Green Canyon Blocks 236 and 237 that could affect EFH and fish resources include (1) coastal and marine environmental degradation, (2) presence of a DP semisubmersible drill rig, (3) temporary discharge of drilling cuttings and associated drilling fluids, and (4) blowouts. Chapters 4.2.1.1.8, 4.2.2.1.10, and 4.4.10 of the Multisale EIS (USDOI, MMS, 2007) contain a discussion of impacts from OCS activity and are hereby incorporated by reference into this PEA.

Drilling fluids and cuttings will be discharged offshore to contribute to localized temporary marine environmental degradation. Drilling operations are restricted in time, and pelagic species in the area could easily avoid discharge plumes. Routine discharges from the DP drilling rig would be highly diluted in the open marine environment.

The presence of the DP drilling rig will temporarily act as a fish attracting device for a short period of time. The anchoring of the FPU is not expected to have any significant impacts on the mud bottom but this structure will act as a fish attracting device for an extended period of time.

Accidental blowouts with associated hydrocarbons also have the potential to affect fish resources and EFH, but there is no evidence that fish or EFH in the Gulf have been adversely affected on a regional population level by spills or chronic contamination. There is less than a 0.5 percent chance of a spill $\geq$ 1,000 bbl occurring and contacting shoreline resources as a result of the proposed Phoenix activities. Fish resources can be affected by oil-spill components that become dissolved, dissipated, and dispersed in the water, and by oil that adheres to particulate matter and sinks into sediment. These effects degrade water and substrate quality, but the impacts are temporary and recoverable. Adult fish will, for the most part, avoid the oil (Malins et al., 1982; NRC, 1985, 2003; Baker et al., 1991). Impacts of oil spills on adult fish have generally been thought to be minimal. Additional discussion of the impacts of oil on fish and fish eggs and larvae can be found in Chapter 4.4.10. of the Multisale EIS (USDOI, MMS, 2007).

In order for an oil spill to affect fish resources at the population level, it would have to be very large and correspond to an area of highly concentrated eggs and larvae. The oil would also have to disperse from the site of a blowout into the water column at levels high enough to cause toxic effects. Given the potential for a blowout, none of these events are likely.

Conclusion

The proposed Phoenix Project, including the drilling of six new wells and the installation of an FPU, is expected to have little impact on any coastal or marine fish, EFH, or commercial fisheries endemic to the northern GOM. If a blowout occurred, plankton, fish eggs, or larvae would suffer mortality in areas where their numbers are concentrated in the upper few meters or feet of water and where oil concentrations are high enough, assuming any oil reached the surface from the bottom. Specific effects from oil spills would depend on several factors, including timing, location, volume and type of oil, environmental conditions, and countermeasures used. Losses from larvae and plankton mortality would take place in 1-2 years by fish from adjacent unaffected areas that replenish larvae in early phases of the life cycle.

3.2.2.4.3. Cumulative Analysis

Principal cumulative impacts on EFH and fish resources include (1) degradation of water quality from oil, fuel, and material spills, high nutrient loads, high turbidity, high BOD, urban runoff, industrial discharges, pathogens, trash and debris, and upriver contaminants; (2) loss of essential habitat important for parts of the life cycle, such as healthy estuarine systems, (including wetland loss); and (3) commercial overfishing. Many of these sources would have little to no impact on the deepwater area of the Phoenix Project. Of these, water quality degradation from multiple inputs and sources, not unique to OCS oil and gas activity, represents the greatest potential for cumulative impacts on fish resources and EFH. Cumulative water quality degradation attributable to OCS oil and gas activity, such as large oil spills, can be dramatic and visually striking when it occurs, but historical data show that that the probability of occurrence is extremely low. Planktonic fish eggs and larvae are more susceptible than adults to environmental contaminants.

Hurricanes may impact fish resources by destroying both coastal wetlands and offshore live-bottom and reef communities and changing physical characteristics of inshore and offshore ecosystems. As a cumulative impacting factor, hurricanes certainly had a substantial impact on Gulf Coast fisheries and EFH in 2005. Contrary to initial fears, however, the majority of significant fishery resource impacts were to the nearshore coastal and wetlands areas of Texas, Louisiana, Mississippi, and Alabama. Hurricanes Katrina and Rita did cause substantial infrastructure (artificial reef EFH) destruction offshore, but the actual impacts to fish resources and EFH were not significant. Hurricanes have essentially no cumulative impacts in deepwater environments such as Green Canyon Blocks 236 and 237.

There would be no cumulative impacts to commercial fishing in the Green Canyon Blocks 236 and 237. There is no commercially viable bottom fishery in the area.

The incremental contribution of the proposed action's impacts to the cumulative impact on fish resources and EFH is negligible and likely undetectable among the other cumulative impacts.

3.2.2.5. Gulf Sturgeon

3.2.2.5.1. Description

The description of the biology, life history, distribution, and causes for population decline of Gulf sturgeon can be found in Chapter 3.2.7.1 of the Multisale EIS (USDOI, MMS, 2007). Designated Gulf sturgeon critical habitat occurs in estuarine and riverine locations along the Gulf Coast east of the Mississippi River in Louisiana, Mississippi, Alabama, and Florida (USDOI, MMS, 2007; Chapter 3.2.7.1). Critical habitat is defined as special geographic areas that are essential for the conservation of a threatened or endangered species and that may require special management and protection. Designated Gulf sturgeon critical habitat is confined to State waters. In addition, there has not been any critical habitat designated in coastal or offshore waters west of the Mississippi River. Therefore, there is no critical habitat within the proposed action area due to the distance from shore and its westward proximity to the Mississippi River. Most activities related to the proposed action will occur in Federal waters (temporary structure placement, exploratory drilling, etc); however, critical habitat may be impacted directly or indirectly.

Various Internet sources were examined to determine any recent information regarding Gulf sturgeon (Florida Fish and Wildlife Commission, 2007; USDOI, FWS, 2007a and b). No new information was discovered from these information sources.

State and Federal resource agencies were contacted and interviews conducted to investigate any recent published or unpublished data that may be available. Current information indicates that there may have been some displacement of sturgeon or possibly damage to their habitat in localized areas where the forces of Hurricane Katrina were the strongest. The current sampling programs along the coastal Gulf South indicate (at least anecdotally) that sturgeon are returning to the areas they occupied prior to the hurricane, which may be indicative of a recovery of those areas (Paruka, personal communication, 2007). No changes in migratory patterns or blockages of migratory pathways have been noted. In general, the researchers noted that the sturgeon are normally found approximately 0.5 mi (0.8 km) from shore between the shoreline and the barrier islands with the bulk of the fish located in the CPA between Petit Bois, Dauphin, and Chandeleur islands and from Perdido to Panama City as far as Fort Walton Beach (Slack, personal communication, 2007; Paruka, personal communication, 2007).

A Gulf sturgeon population census was conducted in the lower Escambia River from October 10 through November 5, 2006. This fish collection coincided with the sturgeons' fall migration from the freshwater to marine environment. This study collected 130 fish ranging in size from 1 to 145 pounds (lb). Large fish (>99 lb) accounted for 10 percent of the catch, which is less than in 2003 where the same class comprised 19 percent of the catch (Paruka, personal communication, 2007). The current Gulf sturgeon population estimate is 451 fish. The decrease from the estimated 554 fish in 2004 is probably a result of the hurricane–induced, degraded water quality.

At present, NOAA indicates that no changes in critical habitat have occurred, and they are working to develop an estimate of sturgeon habitat loss and a habitat suitability index for the species (Bolden, personal communication, 2007). Critical habitat is defined as special geographic areas that are essential for the conservation of a threatened or endangered species and that may require special management and protection. There is also no data indicating that sturgeons are using the deeper Gulf waters. In general, mud substrates found in Gulf waters do not support the appropriate benthic food source for Gulf sturgeon. Based on the absence of critical habitat, lack of preferred substrate, and water depth in the proposed exploration, construction, and well site, there would be minimal to no chance of impacting Gulf sturgeon at the Phoenix Project site.

3.2.2.5.2. Impact Analysis

A detailed impact analysis of the routine, accidental and cumulative impacts of the proposed action on Gulf sturgeon can be found in Chapters 4.2.2.1.9.1, 4.4.9.1, and 4.5.9.1 of the Multisale EIS (USDOI, MMS, 2007).

Impact-producing factors associated with routine exploration activities proposed here could include disturbance of sea bottom with drilling, structure placement, and degradation of estuarine and marine water quality by nonpoint runoff from marine OCS-related facilities, oil or condensate spills associated with a well blowout, vessel traffic, and pipeline installation. Due to the distance of the proposed activity from the nearest shoreline (91 mi; 146 km) and the critical habitat, it is unlikely that offshore spills or effluents will impact Gulf sturgeon habitat. The dilution and low toxicity of this pollution is expected to result in negligible impact of the proposed action on Gulf sturgeon if it does reach the nearshore waters. Vessel traffic will generally only pose a risk to Gulf sturgeon when leaving and returning to port; however, Port Fourchon is outside of this habitat. Major navigation channels are excluded from critical habitat. The Gulf sturgeon's characteristics of bottom-feeding and general avoidance of disturbance make the probability of vessel strike extremely remote. State waters east of the mouth of the Mississippi River have the greatest potential for Gulf sturgeon occurrence and are also the location of its critical habitat. Most of the activities related to the proposed action will occur in Federal waters (e.g., structure placement, drilling, use of existing pipelines, etc.) west of the Mississippi River; therefore, while the potential for direct impact to the sturgeon or its habitat is minimal to none, some indirect impacts could occur but are unlikely.

The most likely accidental impact-producing factor on Gulf sturgeon resulting from the proposed action is an oil spill resulting from a well blowout. Due to the distance of the exploration activity from shore, any oil reaching those areas would be sufficiently weathered to have a minimal toxic effect on the sturgeon. No long-term effects are expected on the size or productivity of any distinct, interbreeding, Gulf sturgeon population stock in the GOM. No coastal spills or blowouts ≥1,000 bbl have occurred from OCS facilities during the historical period of record from 1985 to 1999 (**Appendix B**).

Gulf sturgeon can take up oil by direct ingestion, ingestion of oiled prey, or the absorption of dissolved petroleum components across gill mucus and gill epithelium; however, liver enzymes of adult fish oxidize soluble hydrocarbons into compounds that are excreted in the urine (Spies et al., 1982), without lethal effects. If behavioral studies of other fish species provide a guideline (Farr et al., 1995; Nevissi and Nakatani, 1990), adult sturgeon are likely to actively avoid an oil spill. Based on the Oil-Spill Risk Analysis results (**Appendix B**), there is a <0.5 percent combined probability of an oil spill reaching coastal waters where Gulf sturgeons or their critical habitat are found.

Conclusion

The proposed Phoenix Project is expected to have little impact on Gulf sturgeon. Based on the recent analysis of spill risk from Phoenix-related activities (**Appendix B**), there is a <0.5 percent chance of an oil spill reaching coastal waters where Gulf sturgeons or their critical habitat are found. Due to the distance of the proposed activities from shore (91 mi; 146 km), any oil reaching those areas would be sufficiently weathered to have the minimal toxic effect on the sturgeon. The greatest danger to the critical habitat and the Gulf sturgeon would be from nearshore, shuttle-tanker collisions or offloading spills (USDOI, MMS, 2001). The historical data from 1985 to 1999 show no spills from either of these types of operations has occurred (**Appendix B**).

3.2.2.5.3. Cumulative Analysis

The Gulf sturgeon and its critical habitat can be cumulatively impacted by activities such as oil spills, alteration and destruction of habitat, degradation of water quality, channel construction, dredging and filling operations, flood control activities, natural catastrophes, commercial fishing, and water management responses to drought conditions. The effects from contact with spilled oil will be sublethal and last for less than 1 month.

Non-OCS operations, such as dredge-and-fill activities and natural catastrophes, indirectly impact Gulf sturgeon through the loss of spawning and nursery habitat. Dredge-and-fill activities occur throughout the nearshore areas of the United States. The activities range in scope from propeller dredging (scarring) by recreational boats to large-scale navigation dredging and fill for land reclamation.

Commercial fishing techniques such as trawling, gill netting, or purse seining, when practiced nonselectively, may impact species other than the target species due to incidental catch. Ongoing inshore alterations such as in stream sand and gravel mining, channelization, dredge-and-fill operations, water diversion, and dams, combined with the construction of coastal restoration projects in nearshore waters, will continue to impact sturgeon habitat. If any of the above were to occur and result in damage to Gulf sturgeon critical habitat, it is expected that the Gulf sturgeon will experience a decline in population sizes and a displacement from their current distribution that will last more than one generation.

At present, there is no Gulf sturgeon critical habitat identified west of the Mississippi River in the planning area for the proposed Phoenix Project in Green Canyon. Therefore, the incremental contribution of the proposed action to the cumulative impact is negligible because, even if the sturgeon should come in of contact with project-specific oil spills, the dosage is expected to be sublethal and last less than 1 month.

The NMFS completed consultation as specified under Section 7 of the ESA on the effects of the 5-year OCS Program (2007-2012) in the CPA and WPA. A Biological Opinion was rendered on June 29, 2007, concurring with MMS that the proposed actions would not adversely impact the endangered Gulf sturgeon or its critical habitat and that no additional mitigation actions other than those already identified and in place would be necessary.

3.2.2.6. *Coastal and Marine Birds*

3.2.2.6.1. Description

Information on coastal and marine birds can be found in Chapter 3.2.6 of the Multisale EIS (USDOI, MMS, 2007) and is hereby incorporated by reference into this PEA and is briefly summarized below. The offshore waters, coastal beaches, and contiguous wetlands of the northeastern GOM are populated by both resident and migratory species of coastal and marine birds. Many species are mostly pelagic and are rarely sighted nearshore. Fidelity to nesting sites varies from year to year along the Gulf Coast (Martin and Lester, 1991). Birds may abandon sites along the northern Gulf Coast because of altered habitat and excessive human disturbance.

Seabirds are a diverse group of birds that spend much of their lives on or over saltwater. Species diversity and overall abundance is highest in the spring and summer and lowest in the fall and winter. Four ecological categories of seabirds have been documented in the deepwater areas of the Gulf: summer migrants (e.g., shearwaters, storm petrels, and boobies); summer residents that breed in the Gulf (e.g., sooty, least, and sandwich tern, and frigate birds); winter residents (e.g., gannets, gulls, and jaegers); and permanent resident species (e.g., laughing gulls and royal and bridled terns) (Hess and Ribic, 2000). Collectively, they live far from land most of the year, roosting on the water surface, except at breeding time when they return to nesting areas along coastlines (Terres, 1991). Seabirds typically aggregate in social groups called colonies; the degree of colony formation varies between species (Parnell et al., 1988). They also tend to associate with various oceanic conditions including specific sea-surface temperatures, salinities, areas of high planktonic productivity, or current activity. Seabirds obtain their food from the sea with a variety of behaviors including piracy, scavenging, dipping, plunging, and surface seizing.

Listed Species of Coastal and Marine Birds

The following coastal and marine bird species that inhabit or frequent the northern GOM coastal areas are protected under the ESA as either endangered or threatened: piping plover, whooping crane, brown pelican, least tern, and bald eagle.

Piping Plover

The piping plover (*Charadrius melodus*) is a migratory shorebird that is native to North America. The piping plover was designated as threatened in December 1985 over its range in the Gulf Coast States. It breeds on the northern Great Plains (especially in open flats along the Missouri River), in the Great Lakes, and along the Atlantic Coast (Newfoundland to North Carolina). It winters on the Atlantic and Gulf Coasts from North Carolina to Mexico and in the Bahamas West Indies. Hypothetically, plovers may have a preferred prey base and/or the substrate coloration provides protection from aerial predators due to camouflage by color matching in specific wintering habitat. Such areas include coastal sand flats and mud flats in proximity to large inlets or passes, which may attract the largest concentrations of piping plovers (Nicholls and Baldassarre, 1990). Similarly, nesting habitat in the north includes open flats. This species remains in a precarious state given its low population numbers, sparse distribution, and continued threats to habitat throughout its range.

Critical habitat is specially managed or protected only in the case of a Federal action. On July 10, 2001, critical habitat was designated for the wintering population of piping plover in 146 areas along approximately 2,700 mi (4,344 km) of the coasts of North Carolina, South Carolina, Georgia, Florida, Alabama, Louisiana, and Texas (USDOI, FWS, 2001).

Critical habitat identifies specific areas that are essential to the conservation of a listed species and that may require special management consideration or protection. The primary constituent needs for the piping plover are those habitat components that are essential for the primary biological needs of foraging, shelter, and roosting.

Whooping Crane

The whooping crane (*Grus americana*) is an omnivorous, wading bird. It formerly ranged from summer breeding grounds within the central Canadian provinces and northern prairie states to southern coastal wintering grounds from central Mexico to the Carolinas (Bent, 1926). Whooping cranes currently exist in three wild populations and at five captive locations (USDOI, FWS, 1994). The only self-sustaining wild population nests in Canada's Northwest Territory and adjacent areas of Alberta and winters in coastal marshes and estuarine habitats along the Texas Gulf Coast.

Brown Pelican

The brown pelican (*Pelicanus occidentalis*) remains endangered (*Federal Register*, 1985) in Louisiana and Mississippi, where it inhabits the coastal areas. It is not federally listed in Florida; rather it is a State species of special concern. It feeds entirely upon fishes captured in coastal waters. Organochlorine pesticide pollution contributed to the endangerment of the brown pelican. In recent years, there has been a marked increase in brown pelican populations along its entire former range. The populations of brown pelicans and their habitat in Alabama, Florida, Georgia, North and South Carolina, and points northward along the Atlantic Coast were removed from the endangered species list in 1985.

The Louisiana Dept. of Wildlife and Fisheries submitted a request to FWS in March 1994 to officially remove the brown pelican from the endangered species list in Louisiana (Louisiana Dept. of Wildlife and Fisheries, 1994). Ten thousand nests and an estimated 25,000 adults were found in a recent Louisiana survey (Patrick, personal communication, 1997).

Least Tern

The teast tern is not considered federally endangered or threatened in coastal areas within 50 mi (80 km) of the Gulf (Patrick, personal communication, 1997). Only the interior nesting colonies are endangered.

Bald Eagle

On June 28, 2007, FWS announced the removal of the bald eagle from the list of threatened and endangered species (USDOI, FWS, 2007c). The FWS will work with State wildlife agencies to monitor eagles for at least 5 years. The bald eagle will continue to be protected by the Bald and Golden Eagle Protection Act and the Migratory Bird Treaty Act.

3.2.2.6.2. Impact Analysis

The impact-producing factors associated with development and production of the Phoenix Project in Green Canyon Blocks 236 and 237 that could affect coastal and marine birds include (1) air emissions, (2) helicopter and service-vessel traffic and noise, (3) lights from the floating production unit, (4) oil spills and oil-spill-response activities, and (5) trash and debris from the floating production unit and service vessels. These impact-producing factors apply to nonthreatened or nonendangered bird species as well as those that are listed. Chapters 4.2.1.1.7 and 4.2.2.1.8 of the Multisale EIS (USDOI, MMS, 2007) contain a discussion of impacts from OCS activity and are hereby incorporated by reference into this PEA, and a brief summary follows.

Operations

The major effects of air pollution on birds include direct mortality, debilitating injury, disease, physiological stress, anemia, hypocalcemic condition, bioaccumulation of air pollutants with associated decrease in resistance to debilitating factors, and population declines (Newman, 1979). Contamination of birds or other wildlife by air emissions can occur in three ways: inhalation, absorption, and ingestion.

Air emissions from the Phoenix Project will have a negligible effect on coastal or marine birds that inhabit or transit the offshore OCS area in Grid 9. Emissions from activities associated with the proposed action would be expected to have minimal effects on offshore air quality because of the prevailing atmospheric conditions, emission heights, and pollutant concentrations. Because of distance to the shoreline, no effects would be expected on onshore air quality that could be deleterious to birds.

Helicopter and service-vessel traffic related to the proposed action could sporadically disturb birds while feeding, resting, nesting, or reproducing, or cause them to abandon nests or preferred habitat onshore. The Federal Aviation Administration (USDOT, FAA, 2004) and corporate helicopter policy state that the specified minimum altitude is 610 m (2,000 ft) when flying over populated areas and biologically sensitive areas such as wildlife refuges and national parks. Bird populations inhabiting the helicopter descent corridor at the Port Fourchon onshore service base could be disturbed. Service vessels would use selected transit corridors and adhere to protocol established by USCG for reduced vessel speeds within these inland areas. The effects of routine service-vessel traffic on coastal and marine birds would be negligible.

No drilling fluids and cuttings would be discharged offshore to possibly contact birds on the water or their food supplies. Produced water is expected to be discharged at the sea bed, and routine discharges from the floating production unit would be highly diluted in the open marine environment.

Seabirds (e.g., laughing gulls and petrels) may be attracted by lights and structures in the remote offshore and may remain to rest and feed in the vicinity of fixed platforms. Coastal and marine birds are commonly observed entangled and snared in floating trash and debris. In addition, many species ingest small plastic debris, either intentionally or incidentally. Such interactions can lead to serious injury and death. The MMS's operating regulations at 30 CFR 250.300 and NTL 2003-G06, "Marine Trash and Debris Awareness and Elimination," prohibit the disposal of equipment, containers, and other materials into offshore waters by lessees. The MARPOL Convention (International Maritime Organization, 2008) prohibits the disposal of any plastics at sea or in coastal waters. Due to the low potential for interaction between coastal and marine birds and project-related debris, effects would not occur or would have negligible impact.

Accidental Events

Contact with spilled oil and oil-contaminated prey may be lethal or have serious long-term impacts on marine birds. Stress and shock can enhance the effects of exposure to oil. The direct oiling of coastal or marine birds in a fresh slick is probably lethal. Contact between birds and a weathered or dissipated slick may lead to sublethal effects. Several mechanisms for long-term impacts can be postulated: (1) sublethal initial exposure to oil causing pathological damage and weakening of body systems or inhibiting reproductive success; (2) chronic exposure to residual hydrocarbons in the environment; (3) ingestion of contaminated prey; and (4) altered prey availability resulting from a spill. Ingestion of oil in food occurred after the oil from the *Exxon Valdez* spill had weathered (Hartung, 1995). Final major impacts to European shags (*Phalacrocorax aristotelis*) from the *Prestige* spill off the coast of Spain probably came a year later from a decimated food supply of fish (Velando et al., 2005).

Pneumonia can occur in oiled birds after they inhale droplets of oil while cleaning their feathers. Exposure to oil can cause severe and fatal kidney damage (Frink and Miller, 1995). Ingestion of oils might reduce the function of the immune system and reduce resistance to infectious diseases (Leighton, 1990). Ingested oil may cause toxic destruction of red blood cells and varying degrees of anemia (Leighton, 1990). It is not clear which, if any, of the pathological conditions noted in necropsies are directly caused by hydrocarbons or are a final effect in a chain of events with oil as the initiating cause followed by an intermediate effect of chronic and generalized stress (Clark, 1984). Low levels of oil could stress birds by interfering with food detection, feeding impulses, predator avoidance, territory definition, homing of migratory species, susceptibility to physiological disorders, disease resistance, growth rates, reproduction, and respiration. Recovery would depend on subsequent in-migration of birds from nearby feeding, roosting, and nesting habitats.

The combined probability of a spill occurring in the area of the proposed action and contacting coastal bird resources within 3, 10, or 30 days is <0.5 percent. Impacts on bird resources from such a spill are expected to be negligible.

Oil-spill cleanup methods often require heavy traffic on beaches and wetland areas, application of oil dispersants and bioremediation chemicals, and the distribution and collection of oil containment booms and absorbent material. The presence of humans, along with boats, aircraft, and equipment, could also disturb coastal birds after a spill. Investigations have shown that oil dispersant mixtures pose a threat to bird reproduction similar to that of oil (Albers, 1979; Albers and Gay, 1982) and may reduce chick survival more than exposure to oil alone. Successful dispersal of a spill would generally reduce the probability of exposure of coastal birds to oil (Butler et al., 1988). It is possible that changes in the size of a breeding population may also be a result of disturbance from increased human activity related to cleanup, monitoring, and research efforts (Maccarone and Brzorad, 1994). A relatively recent study states that long-term rigorous studies of rehabilitated and released birds of various species relative to unoiled birds are needed (Russell et al., 2003). Deterrent or preventative methods such as scaring birds from the path of an approaching oil slick or using booms to protect sensitive colonies in an emergency produce mixed results, depending on methods (Clark, 1984). Birds may habituate to the scare if it is always present. A new method of using unmanned (less expensive) scare techniques uses radar to detect the approach of birds. The deterrent device is set off only when birds are detected near a spill (Ronconi et al., 2004).

Conclusion

The proposed Phoenix Project is expected to have little impact on the vitality of any coastal or marine birds or productivity of any population endemic to the northern GOM. It is expected that impacts on coastal and marine birds would be sublethal, consisting of behavioral changes and temporary disturbances or displacement of localized groups. Chronic stress such as digestive distress or occlusion, sublethal ingestion, and behavioral changes, however, are often difficult to detect or attribute. Such stresses can weaken individuals and make them more susceptible to infection and disease as well as making migratory species less fit for migration. Recovery would take place in a period of months to 1 year by the cessation of a disturbance and by the influx of birds from nearby feeding, roosting, and nesting habitats that are unaffected. Impacts to coastal bird resources from an oil spill in the area of the proposed action have a very low probability of occurrence and are therefore expected to be negligible.

3.2.2.6.3.   Cumulative Analysis

Cumulative impacts on coastal and marine birds include (1) air emissions; (2) water quality degradation from oil, fuel, and material spills, high nutrient loads, high turbidity, high BOD, urban runoff, industrial discharges, pathogens, and upriver contaminants; (3) habitat loss and shoreline modification from construction and development; (4) collisions with aircraft; (5) noise from aircraft and vessels; (6)

trash and debris; and (7) natural phenomena such as sea-level rise, subsidence, global warming, and storms and hurricanes. Non-OCS industrial, commercial, or recreational activities that contribute to these cumulative impacts involve the same impact-producing factors as OCS activities. The cumulative impacts from the majority of impact-producing factors on coastal and marine birds would be rarely lethal and predominantly sublethal, constituting behavioral changes, temporary disturbances, or displacement of localized bird groups.

Industry activity that contributes to habitat modification and destruction includes construction and maintenance of pipelines and corridors, and dredging to accommodate deep-draft service vessels used to support deepwater projects. Non-OCS activity would include coastal development, shoreline modifications, flood control programs, and dredging, which would be done to accommodate international shipping and cruise ship traffic.

Exposure to contaminants or discarded debris will usually cause behavioral changes, temporary disturbances, or displacement of localized bird groups. The rates of air and water degradation in coastal and marine environments and the amount of shoreline trash and debris is likely to increase slowly in line with regional economic and population growth trends. Behavioral changes can be expected as competition increases among bird groups for favored habitats. The trash and debris burden on shorelines that is attributable to OCS activity is expected to decline because of continuing education programs for offshore workers, enforcement of controls for trash produced offshore and on service vessels, and industry sponsorship and participation in "beach sweeps" to assay the types of trash found along shorelines and remove it.

Helicopter traffic will increase slightly but will not present an increased collision hazard because these occurrences are rare even now. Aircraft or vessel traffic could sporadically disturb feeding, resting, or nesting behavior of birds or cause abandonment of preferred habitat.

Accidental events, such as an oil spill, would cause lethal effects in birds that are heavily oiled. Coastal birds can be vulnerable to spills making landfall. Contact with weathered oil or a dissipated slick, dispersant chemicals, and spill-response activities in wetlands and other biologically sensitive coastal habitats would be expected to cause lethal to sublethal effects to individuals from any or all bird groups through ingestion or inhalation of oil, ingestion of oiled prey, or food being unavailable because of a spill. Large spills are extremely rare events, and for this reason little or no contact or interaction is expected between birds and freshly spilled oil. Incidental contact with degraded or weathered oil could be expected between birds that inhabit or migrate through Grid 9 over the next 5 years.

The incremental contribution of the proposed Phoenix Project to the cumulative impact would be negligible because the effects of the most likely impacts, such as the physical presence and operation of the platform facility, or noise from helicopters and service-vessel traffic, would only be expected to modify the behavior of birds that come into contact with these project facilities.

The cumulative effects of habitat modification or loss due to onshore commercial, industrial, agricultural and residential development (non-OCS related) may cause an eventual decline or alteration in species density, composition or distribution of avian species typical of coastal regions over a 5-year period. Some of these changes may become permanent, as documented in historical census data, and stem from a net decrease in preferred habitat.

3.3. SOCIOECONOMIC AND HUMAN RESOURCES

3.3.1. Socioeconomic Resources

Socioeconomic resources in the GOM region are characterized in Chapter 3.3 of the Multisale EIS (USDOI, MMS, 2007) and are hereby incorporated by reference into this PEA. Summaries of these resources follow and include (1) the impact area for the proposed Phoenix Project, (2) commercial fisheries, (3) recreational resources, and (4) archaeological resources.

3.3.1.1. Socioeconomic Impact Area

The MMS defines the GOM impact area for population, labor, and employment as that portion of the GOM coastal zone whose social and economic well-being (population, labor, and employment) is directly or indirectly affected by the OCS oil and gas industry. For this analysis, the coastal impact area consists of 132 counties and parishes along the U.S. portion of the GOM. This area includes 42 counties in Texas, 32 parishes in Louisiana, 7 counties in Mississippi, 8 counties in Alabama, and 43 counties in Florida, which are listed in Table 3-17 and illustrated in Figure 3-12 of the Multisale EIS (USDOI, MMS, 2007). Thirteen economic impact areas (EIA's) divide the impact area for analysis purposes and are considered in Chapters 3.3.1 and 3.3.2 of the Multisale EIS (USDOI, MMS, 2007) as the economic impact area for the proposed Phoenix Project.

The criteria for including counties and parishes in this impact area are explained in Chapter 3.3.5.1 of the Multisale EIS (USDOI, MMS, 2007). This impact area is based on sets of counties (and parishes in Louisiana) that have been grouped on the basis of intercounty commuting patterns. The labor market area's (LMA's) identified by this grouping are commuting zones, as identified by Tolbert and Sizer (1996). In their research, Tolbert and Sizer (1996) used journey-to-work data from the 1990 census to construct matrices of commuting flows from county to county. A statistical procedure known as hierarchical cluster analysis was employed to identify counties that were strongly linked by commuting flows. The researchers identified 741 of these commuting zones for the U.S. Twenty-three of these LMA areas span the Gulf Coast, from the southern tip of Texas to Miami and the Florida Keys, and comprise the 13 MMS-defined EIA's for the Gulf.

The socioeconomic resources evaluated in this PEA are limited to that portion of the GOM's coastal zone directly or indirectly affected by activities associated with the Phoenix Project.

3.3.1.2. Commercial Fisheries

3.3.1.2.1. Description

The most recent, complete information on landings and value of fisheries for the U.S. was compiled by NOAA Fisheries Service for 2006. These statistics were reviewed in depth by MMS in the Supplemental EIS for the addition of the 181 South Area to the CPA (USDOI, MMS, 2008). In summary, during 2006, commercial landings of all fisheries in the GOM totaled nearly 1.3 billion pounds, valued at over $662 million (USDOC, NMFS, 2007). The GOM provides over 31 percent of the commercial fish landings in the continental U.S. (excluding Alaska) on an annual basis. Menhaden was the most important GOM species in terms of quantity landed, and shrimp was the most important GOM species in terms of value.

Historically, the deepwater offshore fishery contributes less than 1 percent to the regional total weight and value (USDOI, MMS, 2001). Target species can be classified into three groups: (1) epipelagic (open waters into which enough light penetrates for photosynthesis) fishes; (2) reef fishes; and (3) invertebrates. The Phoenix Project and Green Canyon Bocks 236 and 237 are beyond the normal depth range of commercial reef fishes and invertebrates.

Epipelagic commercial fishes are widespread in the Gulf and assuredly occur in Green Canyon Blocks 236 and 237. Oceanic pelagic fishes were not landed in high quantities overall in the Gulf relative to other finfish groups.

3.3.1.2.2. Impact Analysis

The impact-producing factors associated with the Phoenix Project in Green Canyon Blocks 236 and 237 that could affect commercial fishing include (1) underwater OCS obstructions, (2) coastal and marine environmental degradation, (3) space-use conflicts, (4) temporary discharge of drilling cuttings, and (5) blowouts or oil spills. Chapters 4.2.1.1.9, 4.2.2.1.11, and 4.4.10 of the Multisale EIS (USDOI, MMS, 2007) contain a detailed discussion of impacts from OCS activity and are hereby incorporated by reference into this PEA.

The most likely objectives for commercial fishing would be epipelagic species that are highly mobile and have the ability to avoid disturbed areas. This fishery is traditionally pursued using a highly mobile longliner fleet. There will be some loss of area available to longline fishing by the installation of the Phoenix FPU and DP semisubmersible, and longlines could become entangled in the platform.

Drilling fluids and cuttings discharged offshore would contribute to localized temporary marine environmental degradation. Chronic, low-level contamination of nearshore and open marine environments is a persistent and recurring event resulting in frequent but nonlethal physiological irritation to those resources that lie within the range of impact.

Spills that contact coastal bays and estuaries have the greatest potential to affect commercial fishery resources by killing large numbers of fish eggs and larvae. If a spill contacts nearshore waters, commercially important migratory species could be affected. Although the quantity of commercial landings of migratory species in the GOM is comparatively small, these species can be of high value. There are no commercially important demersal fish resources in the water depths of Green Canyon Blocks 236 and 237.

An unlikely blowout or oil spill ($\geq$1,000 bbl) would be recovered offshore, and what is not recovered would arrive inshore in a highly weathered and degraded state. The impacts of a spill are discussed in detail in Chapter 4.4.10 of the Multisale EIS (USDOI, MMS, 2007). In summary, adult fish must become exposed to crude oil for some time, probably on the order of several months, to sustain a dose that causes biological damage (Payne et al., 1988). Adult fish also possess some capability for metabolizing oil (Spies et al., 1982). Farr et al. (1995) documented an avoidance reaction by fish to waters containing dissolved hydrocarbon, and analogous behavior can be expected of commercially important fish.

Besides the risk of contact from an offshore spill, Louisiana coastal waters could experience a spill along pipelines or vessel transit routes and corridors and near ports that support the proposed operations. According to USCG, 95 percent of all reported coastal spills each year are <24 bbl, so the great majority of coastal spills would likely be small, would disperse quickly, and would have no discernable effect on commercial fisheries. The MMS assumes that a degraded petroleum spill from OCS activity will occasionally contact and affect nearshore and coastal areas of migratory Gulf fisheries. There is no evidence that commercial fisheries in the Gulf have been adversely affected on a regional population level by spills or chronic contamination.

Even if fish resources successfully avoid spills, tainting (oily-tasting fish), public perception of tainting, or the potential of tainting commercial catches will prevent fishermen (either voluntarily or imposed by regulation) from operating in a spill area. Restrictions on catch could decrease landings and/or value for several months. Because the ranges of commercially important fish resources are large, Gulf fishermen do not fish in one locale and have responded to past petroleum spills by moving elsewhere for a few months without substantial loss of catch or income. The effect of oil spills on commercial fishing is expected to have minimal impact on landings, or value of those landings. Potential effects caused by the level of activity of the Phoenix Project would be indistinguishable from variations due to natural causes.

Conclusion

There will be no loss of fishing space because of the physical presence of the structure since it is in an area in which longline commercial fishing is currently banned. In addition, there are no commercially important demersal species at the water depth of this proposed action.

The proposed Phoenix Project is expected to have little impact on the productivity of any commercial fisheries endemic to the northern GOM. There are no commercial fisheries that are restricted exclusively to Green Canyon Blocks 236 and 237. Bottom obstructions are not expected to be an issue because of extreme water depths and the lack of commercially important species at these depths.

Desirable pelagic fish species may also be attracted to the DP semisubmersible drilling rig for the temporary period of operations and could briefly improve commercial catches using fishing techniques other than longlining. A large oil spill, which is unlikely, might adversely affect commercial resources in the general area, but Gulf fishing fleets can respond by temporarily moving the location of their operations.

3.3.1.2.3. Cumulative Analysis

Cumulative impacts on commercial fisheries are the same as on fish resources in general and on EFH as discussed in detail in Chapter 4.5.10 of the Multisale EIS (USDOI, MMS, 2007). These impacts include (1) degradation of water quality from oil, fuel, and material spills, high nutrient loads, high turbidity, high BOD, urban runoff, industrial discharges, pathogens, trash and debris, and upriver contaminants; (2) loss of essential habitat important for parts of a fishery's life cycle, such as healthy estuarine systems (including wetland loss); and (3) overfishing.

Impact-producing factors of the cumulative scenario that are expected to substantially affect commercial fishing include commercial and recreational fishing techniques or practices, hurricanes, installation of production platforms in the future, additional underwater OCS obstructions, seismic surveys, petroleum spills, subsurface blowouts, and offshore discharges of drilling muds and produced waters. At the estimated level of cumulative impact, the resultant influence on commercial fishing,

49

landings, and value of those landings is not expected to be substantial due to the remote location of Green Canyon Blocks 236 and 237 and extreme water depths.

The incremental contribution of the proposed action's impacts to the cumulative impact on commercial fishing is negligible and likely undetectable among the other cumulative impacts.

3.3.1.3. Recreational Resources

3.3.1.3.1. Description

Chapters 3.3.2 and 3.3.3 of the Multisale EIS (USDOI, MMS, 2007) contains a detailed description of recreational resources and is hereby incorporated by reference into this PEA, and a brief summary follows. The northern GOM coastal zone is one of the major recreational regions of the U.S., particularly in connection with marine fishing and beach-related activities. The shorefronts along the Gulf Coasts of Florida, Alabama, Mississippi, Louisiana, and Texas offer a diversity of natural and developed landscapes and seascapes. The coastal beaches, barrier islands, estuarine bays and sounds, river deltas, and tidal marshes are extensively and intensively used for recreational activity by residents of the Gulf South and tourists from throughout the Nation, as well as from foreign countries. Publicly owned and administered areas (such as national seashores, parks, beaches, and wildlife lands), as well as specially designated preservation areas (such as historic and natural sites and landmarks, wilderness areas, wildlife sanctuaries, and scenic rivers), attract residents and visitors throughout the year. Commercial and private recreational facilities and establishments (such as resorts, marinas, amusement parks, and ornamental gardens) also serve as primary interest areas and support services for people who seek enjoyment from the recreational resources associated with the GOM. The Multisale EIS was issued prior (2002) to the impacts of Hurricanes Katrina and Rita (2005), which caused extensive adverse impact to tourism and recreation throughout the Gulf. It will likely take years for tourism and recreation to return to pre-hurricane levels. The MMS has reexamined the analysis for recreational resources in light of these changes. No new information was discovered that would alter the conclusions presented in the Multisale EIS.

3.3.1.3.2. Impact Analysis

The impact-producing factors associated with development and production of the Phoenix Project in Grid 9 that could affect recreational resources includes trash and debris, blowouts, and spilled oil. Chapters 4.2.1.1.10 through 4.2.1.1.13 of the Multisale EIS (USDOI, MMS, 2007) contain a discussion on impacts from OCS activity on recreational fishing and recreational resources and are hereby incorporated by reference into this PEA.

Millions of annual visitors attracted to the coast are responsible for thousands of local jobs and billions of dollars in regional economic activity. Most recreational activity occurs along shorelines and includes such activities as beach use, boating and marinas, camping, water sports, recreational fishing, and bird watching. The location of the Phoenix Project precludes any visual impacts on people engaged in activity along the shoreline or in coastal waters.

Very few recreational fishing trips go into deep water >100 mi (160 km) from shore and beyond the 200-m (656-ft) isobath (the edge of the continental shelf). No impacts would be expected on recreational fishing.

The oil and gas industry is not the main source for trash and debris that litters shorelines along the Gulf. People engaged in recreational activities along the coast are mainly responsible for this litter, as well as trash and debris originating onshore but ending up in the sea through deliberate or careless acts. Other sources of trash and debris include (1) accidental loss from staffed structures in State and Federal waters where hydrocarbons are produced, (2) commercial shrimping and fishing, (3) runoff from storm drains, (4) antiquated storm and sewage systems in older cities, and (5) commercial and recreational fishermen who discard plastics. The U.S. National Park Service documented the origins of trash and debris on South Padre Island in Texas. About 13 percent of the 63,000+ items collected were attributable to the offshore oil and gas industry (Miller and Echols, 1996).

Spills that occur from Phoenix Project activity would be few (if any), volumetrically small, and located near project activities if they did occur. Should a blowout or large (≥1,000 bbl) oil spill occur, the likelihood of contact with shoreline resources is very small. Should one make landfall, it could present aesthetic impacts, but it is likely to be in a degraded state. Recreational beaches may be temporarily closed during cleanup and displace and inconvenience recreational users for up to 1 year. Smaller spills would be subject to weathering and dispersion and would dissipate before landfall.

Conclusion

The proposed Phoenix Project is expected to have little impact on recreational resources. The risk of a large oil spill occurring because of the proposed development operations is very small. The displacements, inconvenience, or closure of recreational resources caused by an oil spill is below the level of social and economic concern. While some accidental loss of solid wastes may occur from the Phoenix Project or service vessels, existing mitigations and regulations that control the handling of offshore trash and debris would be expected to restrict these inputs so that they have a negligible impact on recreational resources.

3.3.1.3.3. Cumulative Analysis

The detailed description of recreational resources in Chapters 3.3.2 and 3.3.3 and the cumulative analysis in Chapters 4.5.12 and 4.5.13 of the Multisale EIS (USDOI, MMS, 2007) address the cumulative effects of OCS and non-OCS impact-producing factors. In the cumulative case, debris and litter derived from both offshore and onshore sources are likely to diminish the tourist potential of beaches and to degrade the ambience of shoreline recreational activities, thereby affecting the enjoyment of recreational beaches throughout the area. The incremental beach trash resulting from the Phoenix Project is expected to be minimal.

Platforms and drilling rigs operating nearshore may affect the ambience of recreational beaches, especially beach wilderness areas. The sound, sight, and wakes of OCS-related and non-OCS-related vessels, as well as OCS helicopter and other light aircraft traffic, are occasional distractions that are noticed by some beach users.

Oil that contacts the coast may preclude short-term recreational use of one or more Gulf Coast beaches at the park or community levels. Displacement of recreational use from impacted areas will occur, and a short-term decline in tourism may result. Beach use at the regional level is unlikely to change from normal patterns; however, closure of specific beaches or parks directly impacted by a large oil spill is likely during cleanup operations. The incremental contribution of the Phoenix Project to the cumulative impact on recreational resources is minor due to the limited effect of increased helicopter, vessel traffic, and marine debris on the number of beach users. The cumulative impact of OCS and State oil and gas activities would be minor.

3.3.1.4. *Archaeological Resources*

3.3.1.4.1. Description

Archaeological resources are any material remains of human life or activity that are at least 50 years old and that are of archaeological interest. The archaeological resources regulation (30 CFR 250.194) provides specific authority to each MMS Regional Director to require archaeological resource surveys, analyses, and reports. Surveys are required prior to any exploration or development activities proposed on leases within the high-probability areas (NTL 2005-G07 and NTL 2006-G07).

Archaeological resources on the OCS can be divided into two types: prehistoric and historic. A detailed description of these resources is provided in Chapter 3.3.4 of the Multisale EIS (USDOI, MMS, 2007).

3.3.1.4.2. Impact Analysis

The impact-producing factors associated with supplemental activities of the Phoenix Project area in Green Canyon Blocks 236 and 237 that could affect archaeological resources include (1) direct contact or disturbance by the installation rig and buoy anchors or mooring chains, (2) ferromagnetic structures or debris on the seabed, (3) onshore development in support of the project, and (4) oil spills. Chapters 4.2.1.1.12, 4.2.2.1.14, 4.4.13, and 4.5.14 of the Multisale EIS (USDOI, MMS, 2007) contain a detailed discussion of impacts (routine, accidental, and cumulative) from OCS activity and are hereby incorporated by reference into this PEA.

The MMS's operational regulation at 30 CFR 250.194 requires that an archaeological survey be conducted prior to development of leases within the high-probability zones for historic and prehistoric archaeological resources. Neither lease block in the proposed Phoenix Project area of Green Canyon are located within MMS's designated high-probability areas for the occurrence of prehistoric or historic archaeological resources. However, recent research on historic shipping routes suggests that Green Canyon Blocks 236 and 237 were located along the historic Spanish trade route, which therefore increases the probability that a historic shipwreck could be located in this area (Lugo-Fernández et al., 2007).

Conclusion

There is no possibility that the proposed Phoenix Project will impact prehistoric archaeological resources because of the extreme water depths.

The proposed Phoenix Project is expected to have no direct or indirect impact on the inventory of known historical shipwrecks located in Green Canyon Blocks 236 and 237. However, impacts are possible on a historic shipwreck because of incomplete knowledge about the location of shipwrecks in the Gulf of Mexico. Direct contact between anchors and mooring lines for OCS surface structures or the emplacement of sea-bottom production structures could destroy or disturb important historic archaeological artifacts or information. Other impact-producing factors would not be expected to adversely affect historic archaeological resources.

3.3.1.4.3. Cumulative Analysis

Green Canyon Blocks 236 and 237 are located in water depths ranging between 600 and 800 m (1,968 and 2,625 ft), precluding the potential for prehistoric sites or artifacts. According to Garrison et al. (1989) and Pearson et al. (2003), the shipwreck database lists no known historic shipwrecks in Green Canyon Blocks 236 and 237.

Construction of new onshore facilities or pipelines in support of OCS activity or coastal development unrelated to OCS activity could result in the direct physical impact to previously unidentified archaeological sites. This direct physical contact with an archaeological site could cause physical damage to, or complete destruction of, information on the prehistory or history of the region and the Nation. Each facility constructed must receive approval from the pertinent Federal, State, county/parish, and/or community involved. Onshore archaeological resources would be protected through the review and approval processes of the various Federal, State, and local agencies involved in permitting onshore activities. A detailed discussion of cumulative impacts from OCS activity can be found in Chapter 3.3.4 of the Multisale EIS and is hereby incorporated by reference into this PEA.

3.3.2. Human Resources and Land Use

Human resources and land use in the WPA are characterized in Chapter 3.3.5 of the Multisale EIS (USDOI, MMS, 2007) and are hereby incorporated by reference into this PEA. Summaries of these resources follow and include (1) population, (2) infrastructure and land use, (3) employment, and (4) environmental justice.

The impacts on human resources and economic activity including (1) population, (2) infrastructure and land use, (3) employment, and (4) environmental justice are discussed in the following sections. Chapters 4.2.1.1.13 and 4.2.2.1.15 of the Multisale EIS (USDOI, MMS, 2007) contain a discussion of impacts on land use, coastal infrastructure, demographics, economic factors, and environmental justice from OCS activity and are hereby incorporated by reference into this PEA.

The human resources and economic activity evaluated in this PEA are limited to that portion of the GOM's coastal zone directly or indirectly affected by OCS development and production in Grid 9. This economic area is concentrated primarily in Texas and Louisiana; however, multiplier effects extend into neighboring states as well. The impacts that result from industry activity on the Federal OCS are taking place in the midst of dynamic commercial and industrial enterprises that move goods and services on Gulf waters and that cause some of the same impact-producing factors as OCS activity.

3.3.2.1. *Population*

3.3.2.1.1. Description

Tables 3-18 through 3-30 of the Multisale EIS (USDOI, MMS, 2007) show baseline population projections for the potential impact areas. Baseline projections are for the impact area in the absence of the proposed activity. These projections include Woods & Poole's assumptions regarding Hurricane Katrina's impact on the Southeast. Table 3-34 of the Multisale EIS (USDOI, MMS, 2007) presents population projections for the eight counties and parishes that were the most negatively affected by Hurricanes Katrina and Rita in terms of population and employment losses: St. Bernard, Orleans, Plaquemines, Jefferson, and Cameron Parishes, Louisiana; and Hancock, Jackson, and Harrison Counties, Mississippi. The analysis area consists of highly populated metropolitan areas (such as the Houston Metropolitan Statistical Area, which dominates Subarea TX-2) and sparsely populated rural areas (as is much of Subarea TX-1). The GOM coastal region's population increased by 19 percent between 1990 and 2000 and by 9 percent between 2000 and 2006. The region's current total population is 23.3 million. In the U.S., population age structures typically reflect the presence of the baby-boom generation. This scenario is manifested in the Gulf Coast region by the relative decline in lower age cohorts over time. More distinctive is the changing race and ethnic composition of the region, which has a long-standing tradition of cultural heterogeneity (Gramling, 1982 and 1996). While the African-American population increased 23.6 percent between 1990 and 2000, the growth rate has declined to 8.2 percent between 2000 and 2006. The Hispanic population increased 53.8 percent between 1990 and 2000 and has continued to increase rapidly since 2000 (24.4%). This group is now the second largest race/ethnic group in the region, making up 25.8 percent of the Gulf Coast population. Although Asians and Pacific Islanders constitute a relatively small proportion of the Gulf Coast population, this group has experienced the highest growth rate between 1990 and 2000 (82.5%) and between 2000 and 2006 (28.2%). The white population has steadily declined and currently constitutes 53.6 percent of the region's population.

3.3.2.1.2. Impact Analysis

No project in Grid 9 is expected to exceed the employment and population impacts associated with the Thunder Horse project in Grid 16. Peak-year direct, indirect, and induced employment impacts associated with development activities proposed for Thunder Horse, the largest development plan proposed to date on the OCS, is projected to be comparable to that projected for the Phoenix Project. Should a project comparable in size and complexity to Thunder Horse occur in Grid 9, population impacts in any given subarea for any given year would still not be expected to exceed 1 percent of the baseline population for any subarea. Minimal effects on population are projected from activities associated with the project. While some of the labor force is expected to be local to the service bases at Port Fourchon and Galveston, most of the additional employees associated with the Phoenix Project are not expected to require local housing.

Conclusion

The proposed Phoenix Project is expected to have a minimal impact on the region's population.

3.3.2.1.3. Cumulative Analysis

As explained in the Multisale EIS (USDOI, MMS, 2007), the Woods & Poole population projections include assumptions concerning the cumulative effects of non-OCS and OCS impacts. Activity from OCS development and production is expected to minimally affect the larger impact areas' demographic patterns or population or education levels but to moderately affect the population levels of local onshore areas where OCS activity is now concentrated. The impact region's population will continue to grow at a slow rate because of general economic development, including OCS activity. Baseline patterns and factors as described in **Chapter 3.3.2** would not be expected to change for the impact area as a whole. Some coastal subareas, Port Fourchon and Galveston, for example, would be expected to experience some impacts due to population growth resulting from increasing demand for OCS labor and deepwater production activity. These impacts could strain local infrastructure, such as schools, roads, hospitals, housing, and city services.

3.3.2.2. Infrastructure and Land Use

3.3.2.2.1. Description

The GOM OCS has one of the highest concentrations of oil and gas activity in the world. The offshore oil and gas industry has experienced dramatic changes over the past two decades. Most of this activity has been concentrated on the continental shelf off the coasts of Texas and Louisiana. The high level of offshore oil and gas activity in the GOM is accompanied by an extensive development of onshore service and support facilities. The major types of onshore infrastructure are described in Chapter 3.3.5.8 of the Multisale EIS (USDOI, MMS, 2007) and include gas processing plants, navigation channels, oil refineries, pipelines and pipeline landfalls, pipecoating and storage yards, platform fabrication yards, service bases, terminals, and other industry-related installations such as landfills and disposal sites for drilling and production wastes; these descriptions are summarized below and are hereby incorporated by reference into this PEA. The vast majority of this infrastructure also supports oil and gas activities in State waters and onshore.

A service base is a community of businesses that load, store, and supply equipment, supplies, and personnel needed at offshore work sites. Although a service base may primarily serve the OCS planning area and subarea in which it is located, it may also provide significant services for the other OCS planning areas and subareas. As OCS operations have progressively moved into deeper waters, larger vessels with deeper drafts (>27 ft or 8 m) have been phased into service mainly for their greater range of travel, greater speed of travel, and larger carrying capacity. Service bases with the greatest appeal for deepwater activity have several common characteristics: (1) a strong and reliable transportation system; (2) adequate depth and width of navigation channels; (3) adequate port facilities; (4) existing petroleum industry support infrastructure; (5) location central to OCS deepwater activities; (6) adequate worker population within commuting distance; and (7) insightful and strong leadership.

Land use in the impact area varies from state to state. Louisiana's coastal impact area is mostly vast areas of wetlands and small communities and industrial areas that extend inland. The coasts of Texas and Florida are a mixture of urban, industrial, recreational beach, wetland, forest, and agricultural areas. Alabama's coastal impact area is predominantly recreational beaches and small residential and fishing communities. Mississippi's coast consists of barrier islands, some wetlands, recreational beaches, and urban areas.

3.3.2.2.2. Impact Analysis

The existing oil and gas infrastructure is expected to be sufficient to handle development associated with the Phoenix Project. The primary onshore support base for operations will be the existing facilities at Port Fourchon, Louisiana. Port Fourchon has a longstanding history servicing offshore oil and gas and is capable of providing the services necessary for the project. It is unlikely that there will be any significant expansions at any existing infrastructure facilities as a result of the proposed activity. No new navigation channels will be required by, and current navigation channels will not change as a result of, the Phoenix Project. Changes in land use throughout the region as a result of the proposed activity would be contained and minimal. While land use in the impact area will change over time, the majority of this change is estimated as general regional growth.

Activities associated with the Phoenix Project are not expected to significantly impact forms of social infrastructure (e.g., schools, hospitals, social services, etc.) in Port Fourchon or any of the other communities in the analysis area. This is due to the minimal population increase expected due to the project (**Chapter 3.3.2.1.2**).

Spills that occur from Phoenix development and production activity would be few (if any), volumetrically small, and located near project activities if they did occur. Should a blowout or large oil spill occur as a result of Phoenix Project activity, the likelihood of contact with shoreline resources is very small. Smaller spills would be subject to weathering and dispersion and would likely dissipate before landfall.

Conclusion

The proposed Phoenix Project is expected to have minimal impact on the region's existing infrastructure or land-use patterns. The existing oil and gas infrastructure is expected to be sufficient to handle development associated with the Phoenix Project. Accidental events such as oil spills and blowouts would have no effects on land use.

3.3.2.2.3. Cumulative Analysis

Much of the cumulative analysis for land use and coastal infrastructure presented in Chapter 4.5.15.1 of the Multisale EIS (USDOI, MMS, 2007) is applicable to the cumulative analysis of Grid 9 and is hereby incorporated by reference into this PEA and is summarized below. This cumulative analysis focuses on the potential direct, indirect, and induced impacts from activities in Grid 9, together with those of other likely future projects (including those under the OCS Program), and trends in the region on coastal infrastructure and land use in those areas. Land use in the analysis area will evolve over time. The majority of this change is estimated as general regional growth rather than activities associated with the OCS Program and State oil and gas activities. Except for the projected new gas processing plants (up to 14 assuming average retirement and no expansions and/or the addition of new capacity to replace what is physically depreciating at all existing facilities) and the 4-6 pipeline shore facilities, the OCS Program will require no new oil and gas coastal infrastructure (USDOI, MMS, 2007). There may be some expansion at current facilities, but the land in the analysis area is sufficient to handle development. There is also sufficient land to construct the projected new gas processing plants and pipeline shore facilities in the analysis area. While it is possible that up to 14 new, greenfield gas processing facilities could be developed, it is much more likely that a large share of the natural gas processing capacity that is needed in the industry will be located at existing facilities, using future investments for expansions and/or to replace depreciated capital equipment. New facilities and expansions would also support State oil and gas production. Thus, the results of OCS and State oil and gas activities are expected to minimally alter the current land use of the area.

Shore-based OCS and State servicing should also increase very slightly in the ports of Galveston, Texas; Port Fourchon, Louisiana; and Mobile, Alabama. There is sufficient land designated in commercial and industrial parks and adjacent to the Galveston and Mobile area ports to minimize disruption to current residential and business use patterns. Port Fourchon, though, has limited land available; operators have had to create land on adjacent wetland areas. Any changes in the infrastructure at Port Fourchon that lead to increases in Louisiana Highway 1 (LA Hwy 1) usage will contribute to the increasing deterioration of the highway. In the absence of the planned expansions, LA Hwy 1 would not be able to handle future OCS and State activities. Additional OCS activity will further strain Lafourche Parish's social infrastructure as well, such as local schools and the water system.

Other ports in the analysis area that have sufficient available land plan to make infrastructure changes. Since the State of Florida and many of its residents reject any mineral extraction activities off their coastline, oil and gas businesses are not expected to be located there.

The incremental contribution of the Phoenix Project to the cumulative impacts on land use and coastal infrastructure are expected to be minor. Of the new coastal infrastructure projected as a result of the OCS Program, none are expected to be constructed as a result of the proposed project. The proposed project would contribute to a very small percentage of the projected OCS-related activity at Port Fourchon.

3.3.2.3. *Employment*

3.3.2.3.1. Description

Table 3-41 of the Multisale EIS (USDOI, MMS, 2007) contains the analysis area's baseline employment projections by MMS-defined EIA. These projections are based on the Woods & Poole's *Complete Economic and Demographic Data Source* (Woods & Poole Economics, Inc., 2006) and assume the continuation of existing social, economic, and technological trends at the time of the forecast. Therefore, the projections include employment associated with the continuation of current patterns in OCS leasing activity as well as the continuation of trends in other industries important to the region. These projections also include Woods & Poole's projections regarding Hurricanes Katrina and Rita's impact on the Southeast.

Average annual employment growth projected from 2005 through 2030 ranges from a low of 1.22 percent for EIA LA-4 to a high of 2.50 percent for EIA FL-1 in the western panhandle of Florida. Over the same time period, employment for the United States is expected to grow at about 1.57 percent per year, while the GOM economic impact analysis area is expected to grow at about 1.73 percent per year. As described above, this represents growth in general employment for the EIA's.

The industrial composition for the EIA's adjacent to the WPA and adjacent to the CPA is similar. In 2005, the top three ranking sectors in terms of employment in all EIA's in the analysis area, except FL-4, were the services, retail trade, and State and local government sectors—with the service industry ranking number one in all EIA's and retail trade ranking second in all EIA's, except FL-2, where State and local government is second. In FL-4, the top three rankings sectors were services; retail trade; and finance, insurances and real estate, in that order, with State and local government a close fourth. In EIA's TX-1, LA-1, LA-3, and FL-2, construction ranks fourth; in EIA's AL-1, MS-1, and TX-2, manufacturing ranks fourth; in EIA's LA-4, TX-3, and FL-3, finance, insurance, and real estate ranks fourth; and in EIA LA-2, mining ranks fourth.

In the Multisale EIS, MMS used data from Woods & Poole's *Complete Economic and Demographic Data Source* (Woods & Poole Economics, Inc., 2006) for baseline population and employment estimates over the 40-year life of a typical proposed CPA lease sale. The 2007 Woods & Poole data became available in late August 2007 and contains their revised estimates regarding the economic and demographic impacts of the 2005 hurricanes on the Gulf region (Woods & Poole Economics, Inc., 2007). In the new data, population, income, and employment declined from 2005 to 2006 by 76 percent in St. Bernard Parish, Louisiana; 51 percent in Orleans Parish, Louisiana; 22 percent in Plaquemines Parish, Louisiana; 19 percent in Cameron Parish; Louisiana; 13 percent in Hancock County, Mississippi; and 11 percent in Harrison County, Mississippi. In each case, these losses were less than those that were in the Woods & Poole 2006 data. The 2007 data also have revised population and employment gains because of Hurricane Katrina displacement: 9 percent in Pearl River County, Mississippi; 7 percent in Tangipahoa Parish, Louisiana; 5 percent in St. John the Baptist Parish, Louisiana; 5 percent in East Baton Rouge Parish, Louisiana; and 4 percent in St. Charles Parish, Louisiana from 2005 to 2006. In each case, these gains were less than those that were in the 2006 data.

Additional supplemental information is available regarding current economic conditions in the GOM region, particularly as it relates the recovery to date from the 2005 hurricanes. However, this new information (summarized below) does not in any way change the baseline population and employment projections used to analyze impacts of a typical CPA sale and the OCS Program, the methodologies used, or the conclusions presented in the Multisale EIS.

More than 2 years after Hurricanes Katrina and Rita the recovery remains uneven throughout the areas originally affected. Areas where the most severe problems remain are Orleans and St. Bernard Parishes, Louisiana; and Hancock County, Mississippi. Affordable housing continues to be a problem in these areas, particularly in New Orleans. Adding to the problem is the high cost of insurance and building materials, causing many prospective developers to postpone projects until these issues are better resolved. Recovery is well underway in Jefferson and Calcasieu Parishes, Louisiana, as well as in Biloxi, Gulfport, and Pascagoula, Mississippi; and Bayou La Batre, Alabama. Recovery is driving expansion in East Baton Rouge and St. Tammany Parishes, Louisiana; Jackson, Hattiesburg, and Laurel, Mississippi; and Gulf Shores and Mobile, Alabama. The measures of recovery are the functions of local government, population, crime, economic and fiscal effects, local government budgets, housing, and labor (Rowley, 2007).

Researchers continue to study the employment impacts of the 2005 hurricane season. The Bureau of Labor Statistics did a special review of the employment impacts of Hurricane Katrina and found that St. Bernard, Orleans, and Jefferson Parishes had the largest percent declines in employment between September 2004 and September 2006 (38%, 27%, and 24.5%, respectively). In the 2 months following Hurricane Katrina, nonfarm payroll employment in Louisiana fell by 241,000, a decline of 12 percent; in the New Orleans metro area, employment declined by 215,000, or 35 percent. In the New Orleans metro area in June 2006, it was 30 percent below the level a year earlier. Total nonfarm employment in Louisiana decreased by 184,600 jobs or 9.6 percent from September 2004 to September 2005, and in May 2006, the year-to-year loss was 177,700 jobs or 9.1 percent (U.S. Dept. of Labor, Bureau of Labor Statistics, 2006; pages 2, 4, 6, 8, 27, and 28). However, more recent data show nonfarm payroll employment in Louisiana increasing 3.8 percent between April 2006 and April 2007 (one of the largest over-the-year percentage gains in employment for a State), or an increase of 69,500 from 1,835,700 to 1,905,200 (U.S. Dept. of Labor, Bureau of Labor Statistics, 2007).

Estimating employment data has proven more difficult post-Katrina, and some previous estimates are being revised as data-gathering limitations are addressed. For example, the Atlanta Federal Reserve Bank announced a revision to their employment estimates for Louisiana from 1,766,400 to 1,844,300 (an increase of 77,900 or 4.4%) between March 2005 and March 2006. Much of the revision was to account for job growth in the State's construction industry that had been underestimated due to survey sampling issues (such as identifying and sampling new construction businesses). Professional and business services is another industry where employment in Louisiana appears to have been originally underestimated (Federal Reserve Bank of Atlanta, 2006).

Researchers also continue to examine the impacts of the 2005 hurricane season on businesses in the region. For example, a Louisiana State University report on the hurricanes' effect on businesses comparing the second quarter of 2005 with the second quarter of 2006 concludes that, after a decline of over 5,000 in the number of employers (5.3%), the entire State of Louisiana had 2,270 fewer employers (2.3%) one year after the hurricanes (Terrell and Bilbo, 2007). The business failure rate in the year after the storms was 11.7 percent for the State as a whole compared with 26.5 percent for the five-parish Southeast region.

3.3.2.3.2. Impact Analysis

The importance of the oil and gas industry to the coastal communities of the GOM is significant, particularly in Louisiana, eastern Texas, and coastal Alabama. This economic analysis focuses on the potential direct, indirect, and induced impacts of the OCS oil and gas industry on the population and employment of the counties and parishes in the impact region.

Peak-year direct, indirect, and induced employment associated with development activities proposed for Thunder Horse in Grid 16, the largest development plan proposed to date on the OCS, was projected at about 1,500 jobs (USDOI, MMS, 2002). Total peak-year employment projections for activities resulting from the Marco Polo project in Grid 13 were comparable with Thunder Horse, 1,565 jobs per year throughout all subareas: 795 direct, 350 indirect, and 420 induced (USDOI, MMS, 2003a). Phased development and production is proposed under the Phoenix Project, with production beginning in 2008 and ending in 2018. The total peak-year employment from the Phoenix Project is not expected to exceed these projects and is expected to occur between 2009 and 2013.

The Phoenix Project is expected to have minimal impacts on employment throughout all 13 of the EIA's identified above in **Chapter 3.3.1.1** (Socioeconomic Impact Area). The majority of employment resulting from the Phoenix Project is expected to occur in EIA's TX-1, TX-2, TX-3, LA-1, LA-2, and LA-3 because of the location of the project and because the oil and gas industry is best established in these areas. Even assuming that all 1,500 jobs would occur in any single EIA in Texas or Louisiana, a highly unlikely scenario but one used to evaluate maximum possible impacts, employment does not exceed 1 percent of the total baseline employment projections for any given EIA during 2009 through 2013. This demand is expected to be met primarily with the existing available labor force.

Should a blowout or large oil spill occur, the likelihood of contact with shoreline resources is very small. Smaller spills would be subject to weathering and dispersion and would likely dissipate before landfall. The potential positive and negative employment impacts of an oil spill are characterized in Chapter 4.4.14.3 of the Multisale EIS (USDOI, MMS, 2007) and are hereby incorporated by reference into this PEA. The net employment impacts of a spill are expected to be minimal.

Conclusion

The proposed Phoenix Project is expected to have minimal impacts on employment in the Texas, Louisiana, Mississippi, Alabama, and Florida EIA's. The project is expected to generate less than a 1 percent increase in employment in any of these subareas.

3.3.2.3.3. Cumulative Analysis

Much of the cumulative analysis for economic factors presented in Chapter 4.5.15.3 of the Multisale EIS (USDOI, MMS, 2007) is applicable to this cumulative employment analysis and is hereby incorporated by reference into this PEA, and is summarized below. This cumulative employment analysis focuses on the potential direct, indirect, and induced employment impacts from activities in Grid 9, together with those of other likely future projects (including those under the OCS Program), and trends in the region. Most approaches to analyzing cumulative effects begin by assembling a list of "other likely projects and actions" that will be included with the proposed action for analysis. However, no such list of future projects and actions could be assembled that would be sufficiently current and comprehensive to support a cumulative analysis for all 132 of the coastal counties and parishes in the analysis area over the time period of analysis. Instead of an arbitrary assemblage of future possible projects and actions, this analysis employs the baseline employment projections from Woods & Poole Economics, Inc. (2007) used above in **Chapter 3.3.2.3.2** to define the contributions of other likely projects, actions, and trends to the cumulative case. These projections represent a more comprehensive and accurate appraisal of cumulative conditions than could be generated using the traditional list of possible projects actions.

The incremental contribution of the Phoenix Project to the cumulative employment impacts are expected to be minor. No project in Grid 9 is expected to exceed the employment impacts associated with the Thunder Horse project in Grid 16. Should a project comparable in size and complexity with Thunder Horse occur in Grid 9, employment impacts in any given subarea for any given year would still not be expected to exceed 1 percent of the baseline employment for any subarea (**Chapter 3.3.2.3.2**).

Employment demand will continue to be met primarily with the existing population and available labor force in most EIA's. The MMS does expect some employment will be met through in-migration; however, this level is projected to be small and localized. Port Fourchon is experiencing full employment, housing shortages, and stresses on local infrastructure—roads (LA Hwy 1), water supply, schools, hospitals, etc. Port Fourchon is a focal point for OCS development, especially deepwater OCS operations. The Port (and the surrounding community and infrastructure) is still experiencing increased activity as a result of the 2005 hurricane season. Any additional employment, particularly new residential employment, and the resultant strain on infrastructure, are expected to have a significant impact on the area. In addition, ports throughout the Gulf are experiencing labor shortages for higher skilled positions as electricians, fitters, crane operators, and boat captains, an issue that existed prior to the 2005 hurricane season. This may lead to additional in-migration to these areas to fill these positions.

3.3.2.4. *Environmental Justice*

3.3.2.4.1. Description

On February 11, 1994, President William J. Clinton issued Executive Order 12898, *Federal Actions to Address Environmental Justice in Minority Populations and Low-Income Populations*, which directs Federal agencies to assess whether their actions have disproportionate environmental effects on people of ethnic or racial minorities or people with low incomes. Those environmental effects encompass human health, social, and economic consequences. The Federal agency in charge of the proposed action must provide opportunities for community input during the NEPA process (See **Chapter 4** for a discussion of consultation and coordination.). There are no environmental justice issues in the actual offshore Gulf of Mexico OCS planning areas; however, environmental justice concerns may be related to nearshore and onshore activities in support of the proposed Phoenix Project. Environmental justice issues are in two categories—those related to routine operations and those related to accidental events. Issues related to routine operations center on increases in onshore activity (such as employment, migration, commuter traffic, and truck traffic) and on additions to or expansions of the infrastructure supporting this activity (such as fabrication yards, supply ports, and onshore disposal sites for offshore waste). Issues related to accidents focus on oil spills.

3.3.2.4.2. Impact Analysis

Federal agencies are directed by Executive Order 12898 to assess whether their actions would have a disproportionate and negative effect on the environment and health of people of ethnic or racial minorities or those with low income. The existing onshore facilities that can support the projected developments within Grid 9 are well established along the Gulf Coast, and no disproportionate impacts on ethnic or racial minorities or poor people would result from their continued operation.

Conclusion

The proposed Phoenix Project is expected to have no impacts on existing equities of environmental justice.

3.3.2.4.3. Cumulative Analysis

Future years may bring expansion or upgrading of existing onshore facilities that support OCS activities in Grid 9, but entirely new development is unlikely. The existing coastal support facilities are well established, and no disproportionate effects on ethnic or racial minorities or poor people would be expected to result from their continued operation. In the GOM coastal area, the contribution of the Phoenix Project to the cumulative effects of all activities and trends affecting environmental justice issues is expected to be negligible to minor. Chapter 4.5.15.4 of the Multisale EIS (USDOI, MMS, 2007) analyzes cumulative environmental justice effects in Lafourche Parish, Louisiana.

4. CONSULTATION AND COORDINATION

Necessary consultation and coordination for this proposed action was conducted during the preparation of the Multisale EIS (USDOI, MMS, 2007). The State of Louisiana has an approved Coastal Zone Management (CZM) Program. Therefore, certificates of coastal zone consistency from the State were required for the proposed activities. The MMS mailed the DOCD and other required and necessary information to the Louisiana Department of Natural Resources for CZM concurrence on January 7, 2008. The State of Louisiana, on January 25, 2008, provided a letter with a Certificate of Coastal Zone Consistency with the State's CZM Program; the letter was received by MMS on January 28, 2008. The MMS published a description of ERT's proposed action in the *Times-Picayune* on January 21, 2008, and the *Houma Courier* on January 21, 2008. The description provided the public with a Notice of Preparation of an EA and outlined the activities ERT proposed for the Phoenix Project. The Notice requested that interested parties submit comments to MMS on issues that should be addressed in the PEA. The 30-day comment period ended on February 20, 2008. No comments were received during this period.

5. REFERENCES

Advanced Research Projects Agency. 1995. Final environmental impact statement/environmental impact report (EIS/EIR) for the California Acoustic Thermometry of Ocean Climate (ATOC) Project and its associated Marine Mammal Research Program (MMRP) (Scientific Research Permit Application [P557A]), Vol. 1.

Aharon, P., D. Van Gent, B. Fu, and L.M. Scott. 2001. Fate and effects of barium and radium-rich fluid emissions from hydrocarbon seeps on the benthic habitats of the Gulf of Mexico offshore Louisiana. U.S. Dept. of the Interior, Minerals Management Service, Gulf of Mexico OCS Region, New Orleans, LA. OCS Study MMS 2001-004. 142 pp.

Albers, P.H. 1979. Effects of Corexit 9527 on the hatchability of mallard eggs. Bull. Environ. Contam. and Toxicol. 23:661-668.

Albers, P.H. and M.L. Gay. 1982. Effects of a chemical dispersant and crude oil on breeding ducks. Bull. Environ. Contam. and Toxicol. 9:138-139.

Alexander, S.K. and J.W. Webb. 1983. Effects of oil on growth and decomposition of *Spartina alterniflora*. In: Proceedings, 1983 Oil Spill Conference. February 28-March 3, 1983, San Antonio, TX. Washington, DC: American Petroleum Institute. Pp. 529-532.

Alexander, S.K. and J.W. Webb. 1987. Relationship of *Spartina alterniflora* growth to sediment oil content following an oil spill. In: Proceedings, 1987 Oil Spill Conference, April 6-9, 1988, Baltimore, MD. Washington, DC: American Petroleum Institute. Pp. 445-450.

Baker, J.M., R.B. Clark, and P.F. Kingston. 1991. Two years after the spill: Environmental recovery in Prince William Sound and the Gulf of Alaska. Institute of Offshore Engineering, Heriot-Watt University, Edinburgh, EH14 4AS, Scotland. 31 pp.

Ballachey, B.E., J.L. Bodkin, and A.R. DeGange. 1994. An overview of sea otter studies. In: Loughlin, T.R., ed. Marine mammals and the *Exxon Valdez*. San Diego, CA: Academic Press. Pp. 47-59.

Barras, J.A. 2006. Land area change in coastal Louisiana after the 2005 hurricanes: A series of three maps. U.S. Dept. of the Interior, Geological Survey. Open-File Report 06-1274. Internet website: http://pubs.usgs.gov/of/2006/1274/.

Barras, J.A. 2007a. Satellite images and aerial photographs of the effects of Hurricanes Katrina and Rita on coastal Louisiana. U.S. Dept. of the Interior, Geological Survey. Geological Survey Data Series 281. Internet website: http://pubs.usgs.gov/ds/2007/281.

Barras, J.A. 2007b. Land area changes in coastal Louisiana after Hurricanes Katrina and Rita. In: Farris, G.S., G.J. Smith, M.P. Crane, C.R. Demas, L.L. Robbins, and D.L. Lavoie, eds. Science and the storms: The USGS response to the hurricanes of 2005. U.S. Dept. of the Interior, Geological Survey. Geological Survey Circular 1306. Pp. 97-112. Internet website: http://pubs.usgs.gov/circ/1306/pdf/c1306_ch5_b.pdf.

Basan, P.B., C.K. Chamberlain, R.W. Frey, J.D. Howard, A. Seilacher and J.E. Warme. 1978. Trace fossil concepts. Society of Economic Paleontologists and Mineralogists, Short Course No. 5, Tulsa, OK. 181 pp.

Bent, A.C. 1926. Life histories of North American marsh birds. New York: Dover Publications.

Bolden, S. 2007. Personal communication. Information concerning the critical habitat and damage assessments of the Gulf sturgeon. U.S. Dept. of Commerce, National Oceanic and Atmospheric Administration, Fisheries Service, St. Petersburg, FL. May 9, 2007.

Brooks, J.M., C. Fisher, H. Roberts, B. Bernard, I. MacDonald, R. Carney, S. Joye, E. Cordes, G. Wolff, and E. Goehring. In press. Investigations of chemosynthetic communities on the lower continental slope of the Gulf of Mexico: Interim report. U.S. Dept. of the Interior, Minerals Management Service, Gulf of Mexico OCS Region, New Orleans, LA. OCS Study MMS 2008-009.

Butler, R.G., A. Harfenist, F.A. Leighton, and D.B. Peakall. 1988. Impact of sublethal oil and emulsion exposure on the reproductive success of Leach's storm-petrels: Short- and long-term effects. Journal of Applied Ecology 25:125-143.

Carr, A. 1987. Impact of nondegradable marine debris on the ecology and survival outlook of sea turtles. Marine Pollution Bulletin 18:352-356.

Carr, A. and D.K. Caldwell. 1956. The ecology and migration of sea turtles. I. Results of field work in Florida, 1955. Amer. Mus. Novit. 1793:1-23.

Chan, E.H. and H.C. Liew. 1988. A review of the effects of oil-based activities and oil pollution on sea turtles. In: Sasekumar, A., R. D'Cruz, and S.L.H. Lim, eds. Thirty years of marine science research and development. Proceedings of the 11th Annual Seminar of the Malaysian Society of Marine Science, 26 March 1988, Kuala Lumpur, Malaysia. Pp. 159-168.

Clark, R.B. 1984. Oiled seabird rescue and conservation. Journal of the Fisheries Research Board of Canada 35:675-678.

Continental Shelf Associates, Inc. 2006. Effects of oil and gas exploration and development at selected continental slope sites in the Gulf of Mexico. Volume II: Technical report. U.S. Dept. of the Interior, Minerals Management Service, Gulf of Mexico OCS Region, New Orleans, LA. OCS Study MMS 2006-045. 636 pp.

Corliss, J.B., J. Dymond, L. Gordon, J.M. Edmond, R.P. von Herzen, R.D. Ballard, K. Green, D. Williams, A. Bainbridge, K. Crane, and T.H. Van Adel. 1979. Submarine thermal springs on the Galapagos Rift. Science 203:1073-1083.

Davis, R.W. and G.S. Fargion, eds. 1996. Distribution and abundance of cetaceans in the north-central western Gulf of Mexico: Final report. Volume II: Technical report. OCS Study MMS 96-0027. 355 pp.

Davis, R.W., W.E. Evans, and B. Würsig, eds. 2000. Cetaceans, sea turtles, and seabirds in the northern Gulf of Mexico: Distribution, abundance and habitat associations. Volume I: Executive summary. U.S. Dept. of the Interior, Geological Survey, Biological Resources Division, USGS/BRD/CR-1999-

0006 and Minerals Management Service, Gulf of Mexico OCS Region, New Orleans, LA, OCS Study MMS 2000-002. 40 pp.

Delaune, R.D., W.H. Patrick, and R.J. Bureh. 1979. Effect of crude oil on a Louisiana *Spartina alterniflora* salt marsh. Environ. Poll. 20:21-31.

Doering, F., I.W. Duedall, and J.M. Williams. 1994. Florida hurricanes and tropical storms 1871-1993: An historical survey. Florida Institute of Technology, Division of Marine and Environmental Systems, Florida Sea Grant Program, Gainesville, FL. Tech. Paper 71. 118 pp.

Ehrhart, L.M. 1978. Choctawhatchee beach mouse. In: Layne, J.N., ed. Rare and endangered biota of Florida. Volume I: Mammals. Gainesville, FL: University Presses of Florida. Pp. 18-19.

Ekdale, A.A., R.G. Bromley and S.G. Pemberton. 1984. Ichnology; the use of trace fossils in sedimentology and stratigraphy. Society of Economic Paleontologists and Mineralogists, Short Course No. 15. Tulsa, OK. 317 pp.

Energy Resource Technology, Inc. (ERT). 2007. Joint supplemental developmental operations coordination document: Lease OCS-G 15562/15563, Green Canyon Blocks 236/237, offshore Louisiana. Energy Resource Technology, Inc., Houston, TX.

Farr, A.J., C.C. Chabot, and D.H. Taylor. 1995. Behavioral avoidance of flurothene by flathead minnows (*Pimephales promelas*). Neurotoxicology and Teratology 17(3):265-271.

Federal Register. 1985. Endangered and threatened wildlife and plants; removal of the brown pelican in the southeastern United States from the list of endangered and threatened wildlife. 50 FR 23.

Federal Reserve Bank of Atlanta. 2006. Louisiana continues to march toward recovery—Louisiana employment: Better than the data suggest. EconSouth 8(4), fourth quarter 2006. Internet website: http://www.frbatlanta.org/invoke.cfm?objectid=A6993158-5056-9F12-12433D9D81C1D2AC&method=display_body. Accessed June 14, 2007.

Fischel, M., W. Grip, and I.A. Mendelssohn. 1989. Study to determine the recovery of a Louisiana marsh from an oil spill. In: Proceedings, 1989 Oil Spill Conference . . . February 13-16, 1989, San Antonio, TX. Washington, DC: American Petroleum Institute. Pp. 383-387.

Fisher, C.R. 1990. Chemoautotrophic and methanotrophic symbioses in marine invertebrates. Reviews in Aquatic Sciences 2:399-436.

Florida A&M University. 1988. Meteorological database and synthesis for the Gulf of Mexico. U.S. Dept. of the Interior, Minerals Management Service, Gulf of Mexico OCS Region, New Orleans, LA. OCS Study MMS 88-0064. 486 pp.

Florida Fish and Wildlife Commission. 2007. Fish and Wildlife Research Institute. Internet website: http://research.myfwc.com/features/view-article.asp?id=3261. Accessed May 29, 2007.

Frey, R.W. 1975. The study of trace fossils; a synthesis of principles, problems, and procedures in ichnology. New York, NY: Springer-Verlag. 562 pp.

Frink, L. and E.A. Miller. 1995. Principles of oiled bird rehabilitation. In: Frink, L., K. Ball-Weir, and C. Smith, eds. Wildlife and oil spills: response, research, and contingency planning. Newark, DE: Tri-State Bird Rescue & Research, Inc.

Fu, B. and P. Aharon. 1998. Sources of hydrocarbon-rich fluids advecting on the seafloor in the northern Gulf of Mexico. Gulf Coast Association of Geological Societies Transactions 48:73-81.

Gallaway, B.J. and M.C. Kennicutt II. 1988. Chapter 2. The characterization of benthic habitats of the northern Gulf of Mexico. In: Gallaway, B.J., ed. Northern Gulf of Mexico Continental Slope Study, Final Report: Year 4. Vol. III: Appendices. U.S. Dept. of the Interior, Minerals Management Service, Gulf of Mexico OCS Region, New Orleans, LA. OCS Study MMS 88-0054. Pp. 2-1 to 2-45.

Gallaway, B.J., L.R. Martin, and R.L. Howard, eds. 1988. Northern Gulf of Mexico continental slope study, annual report: Year 3. Volume II: Technical narrative. U.S. Dept. of the Interior, Minerals

Management Service, Gulf of Mexico OCS Region, New Orleans, LA. OCS Study MMS 87-0060. 586 pp.

Gallaway, B.J., J.G. Cole and R.G. Fechhelm. 2003. Selected aspects of the ecology of the continental slope fauna of the Gulf of Mexico: A synopsis of the northern Gulf of Mexico continental slope study, 1983-1988. U.S. Dept. of the Interior, Minerals Management Service, Gulf of Mexico OCS Region, New Orleans, LA. OCS Study MMS 2003-072. 38 pp. + apps.

Garrison, E.G., C.P. Giammona, F.J. Kelly, A.R. Tripp, and G.A. Wolf. 1989. Historic shipwrecks and magnetic anomalies of the northern Gulf of Mexico: Reevaluation of archaeological resource management zone 1. U.S. Dept. of the Interior, Minerals Management Service, Gulf of Mexico OCS Region, New Orleans, LA. OCS Study MMS 89-0024. 241 pp.

Geraci, J.R. and D.J. St. Aubin. 1980. Offshore petroleum resource development and marine mammals: A review and research recommendations. Marine Fisheries Review 42:1-12.

Gramling, R.B. 1982. Cultural history of the Atchafalaya Basin, 1900 to the present. In: Gibson, J.L., ed. Archeology and ethnology on the edges of the Atchafalaya Basin, south central Louisiana, a cultural resources survey of the Atchafalaya basin protection levees: Final report. U.S. Dept. of the Army, Corps of Engineers, New Orleans District, New Orleans, LA. PD-RC-82-04. Pp. 109-151.

Gramling, R.B. 1996. Oil on the edge: Offshore development, conflict, gridlock. Albany, NY: State University of New York Press. 208 pp.

Gulf of Mexico Fishery Management Council (GMFMC). 2005. Generic amendment number 3 for addressing essential fish habitat requirements, habitat areas of particular concern, and adverse effects of fishing in the following fishery management plans of the Gulf of Mexico: Shrimp fishery of the Gulf of Mexico, United States waters red drum fishery of the Gulf of Mexico, reef fish fishery of the Gulf of Mexico, coastal migratory pelagic resources (mackerels) in the Gulf of Mexico, and South Atlantic stone crab fishery of the Gulf of Mexico, spiny lobster in the Gulf of Mexico, and South Atlantic coral and coral reefs of the Gulf of Mexico. Gulf of Mexico Fishery Management Council, Tampa, FL.

Hartung, R. 1995. Assessment of the potential for long-term toxicological effects of the *Exxon Valdez* oil spill on birds and mammaals. In: Wells, P.G., J.N. Butler, and J.S. Hughes, eds. *Exxon Valdez* oil spill fate and effects in Alaskan waters. Philadelphia, PA: American Society for Testing and Materials. ASTM STP No. 1219.

Harvey, J.T. and M.E. Dahlheim. 1994. Cetaceans in oil. In: Loughlin, T.R., ed. Marine mammals and the *Exxon Valdez*. San Diego, CA: Academic Press. Pp. 257-264.

Hess, N.A. and C.A. Ribic. 2000. Seabird ecology. Chapter 8. In: Davis, R.W., W.E. Evans, and B. Wursig, eds. Cetaceans, sea turtles and seabirds in the northern Gulf of Mexico: Distribution, abundance and habitat associations. Volume II: Technical report. U.S. Dept. of the Interior, Geological Survey, Biological Resources Division, USGS/BRD/CR-1999-0006 and the Minerals Management Service, Gulf of Mexico OCS Region, New Orleans, LA, OCS Study MMS 2000-003. 364 pp.

International Maritime Organization. 2008. International Convention for the Prevention of Pollution from Ships, 1973, as modified by the Protocol of 1978 relating thereto (MARPOL 73/78). Internet website: http://www.imo.org/Conventions/mainframe.asp?topic_id=258&doc_id=678. Accessed February 27, 2008.

Jochens, A., D. Biggs, K. Benoit-Bird, D. Engelhardt, J. Gordon, C. Hu, N. Jaquet, M. Johnson, R. Leben, B. Mate, P. Miller, J. Ortega-Ortiz, A. Thode, P. Tyack, and B. Würsig. 2008. Sperm whale seismic study in the Gulf of Mexico: Synthesis report. U.S. Dept. of the Interior, Minerals Management Service, Gulf of Mexico OCS Region, New Orleans, LA. OCS Study MMS 2008-006.

Kennicutt, M.C., J. Sericano, T. Wade, F. Alcazar, and J.M. Brooks. 1987. High-molecular weight hydrocarbons in the Gulf of Mexico continental slope sediment. Deep-Sea Research 34:403-424.

Leighton, F.A. 1990. The toxicity of petroleum oils to birds: An overview. Oil Symposium, Herndon, VA.

LGL Ecological Research Associates, Inc. and Science Applications International Corporation. 1998. Cumulative ecological significance of oil and gas structures in the Gulf of Mexico: Information search, synthesis, and ecological modeling. Phase I, final report. U.S. Dept. of the Interior, Minerals Management Service, Gulf of Mexico OCS Region, New Orleans, LA. OCS Study MMS 97-0036. 130 pp.

Louisiana Coastal Wetlands Conservation and Restoration Task Force. 1993. Coastal Wetland Planning, Protection, and Restoration Act: Louisiana coastal wetlands restoration plan; main report and environmental impact statement. Louisiana Coastal Wetlands Conservation and Restoration Task Force, Baton Rouge, LA.

Louisiana Dept. of Wildlife and Fisheries. 1994. A fisheries management plan for Louisiana penaeid shrimp fishery: Summary and action items. November 1992, Baton Rouge, LA. 16 pp.

Louisiana Dept. of Wildlife and Fisheries, Fur and Refuge Division, and the U.S. Dept. of the Interior, Geological Survey, Biological Resources Division. 1997. Louisiana coastal marsh vegetative type map (database). Louisiana Dept. of Wildlife and Fisheries, Fur and Refuge Division, and the U.S. Geological Survey's National Wetlands Research Center, Lafayette, LA.

Louisiana Sea Grant. 2005. Louisiana hurricane recovery resources (LHRR). Internet website: http://www.laseagrant.org/hurricane/oil.htm. Accessed March 30, 2006.

Lugo-Fernández, A., D.A. Ball, M. Gravois, C. Horrell, and J.B. Irion. 2007. Analysis of the Gulf of Mexico's Veracruz-Havana route of *La Flota de la Nueva España*. Journal of Maritime Archaeology 2:24-47.

Lytle, J.S. 1975. Fate and effects of crude oil on an estuarine pond. In: Proceedings, Conference on Prevention and Control of Oil Pollution, San Francisco, CA. Pp. 595-600.

Maccarone, A.D. and J.N. Brzorad. 1994. Gulf and waterfowl populations in the Arthur Kill. In: Burger, J., ed. Before and after an oil spill: The Arthur Kill. New Brunswick, NJ: Rutgers University Press. Pp. 595-600.

MacDonald, I.R., ed. 1992. Chemosynthetic ecosystems study literature review and data synthesis, northern Gulf of Mexico: Volumes I-III. U.S. Dept. of the Interior, Minerals Management Service, Gulf of Mexico OCS Region, New Orleans, LA. OCS Study MMS 92-0033, 92-0034, and 92-0035. 25, 218, and 263 pp., respectively.

MacDonald, I.R., ed. 1998. Stability and change in Gulf of Mexico chemosynthetic communities: Interim report. U.S. Dept. of the Interior, Minerals Management Service, Gulf of Mexico OCS Region, New Orleans, LA. OCS Study MMS 98-0034. 114 pp.

MacDonald, I.R., N.L. Guinasso Jr., S.G. Ackleson, J.F. Amos, R. Duckworth, R. Sassen, and J.M. Brooks. 1993. Natural oil slicks in the Gulf of Mexico visible from space. J. Geophys. Res. 98(C9):16,351-16,364.

Malins, D.C., S. Chan, H.O. Hodgins, U. Varanasi, D.D. Weber, and D.W. Brown. 1982. The nature and biological effects of weathered petroleum. U.S. Dept. of Commerce, National Marine Fisheries Service, Northwest and Alaska Fisheries Center, Environmental Conservation Division, Seattle, WA. 43 pp.

Martin, R.P., and G.D. Lester. 1991. Atlas and census of wading bird and seabird nesting colonies in Louisiana: 1990. Special Publication No. 3, Louisiana Dept. of Wildlife and Fisheries, Louisiana Natural Heritage Program.

Miller, J.E. and D.L. Echols. 1996. Marine debris point source investigation: Padre Island National Seashore, March 1994-September 1995. U.S. Dept. of the Interior, Minerals Management Service, Gulf of Mexico OCS Region, New Orleans, LA. OCS Study MMS 96-0023. 35 pp.

Mitchell, R. 2000. Scientists find that tons of oil seep into the Gulf of Mexico each year. U.S. Dept. of Commerce, National Atmospheric and Science Administration, Earth Observatory, Silver Springs, MD. Internet website: http://www.earthobservatory.nasa.gov/Newsroom/MediaAlerts/2000/200001261633.html. Accessed January 26, 2002.

Mitchell, R., I.R. MacDonald, and K.A. Kvenvolden. 1999. Estimation of total hydrocarbon seepage into the Gulf of Mexico based on satellite remote sensing images. Transactions, American Geophysical Union 80(49), Ocean Sciences Meeting, OS242.

Miller, T.L., R.A. Morton, A.H. Sallenger, and L.J. Moore. 2004. The national assessment of shoreline change: A GIS compilation of vector shorelines and associated shoreline change data for the U.S. Gulf of Mexico. U.S. Dept. of the Interior, Geological Survey. Geological Survey Open-File Report 2004-1089. Internet website: http://pubs.er.usgs.gov/usgspubs/ofr/ofr20041089. Accessed May 2007.

Moyers, J.E. 1996. Food habits of Gulf Coast subspecies of beach mice (*Peromyscus polionotus* spp.). M.S. Thesis, Auburn University, AL. 84 pp.

Murray, S.P. 1998. An observational study of the Mississippi/Atchafalaya coastal plume: Final report. U.S. Dept. of the Interior, Minerals Management Service, Gulf of Mexico OCS Region, New Orleans, LA. OCS Study MMS 98-0040. 513 pp.

National Research Council (NRC). 1985. Oil in the sea—inputs, fates and effects. Washington, DC: National Academy Press. 601 pp.

National Research Council (NRC). 1990. Decline of the sea turtles: Causes and prevention. Committee on Sea Turtle Conservation. Washington, DC: National Academy Press. 280 pp.

National Research Council (NRC). 2003. Oil in the sea III: Inputs, fates, and effects. Washington, DC: National Academy Press. 265 pp.

Neumann, C.J., B.R. Jarvinen, and J.D. Elms. 1993. Tropical cyclones of the north Atlantic Ocean, 1871-1992. U.S. Dept. of Commerce, National Oceanic and Atmospheric Administration, Asheville, NC. 193 pp.

Nevissi, A.E. and R.E. Nakatani. 1990. Effect of Prudhoe Bay oil on the homing of Coho salmon in marine waters. Journal of Fish Biology 34:621-629.

New England River Basins Commission (NERBC). 1976. Factbook. In: Onshore facilities related to offshore oil and gas development. Boston, MA.

Newman, J.R. 1979. Effects of industrial air pollution on wildlife. Biol. Conserv. 15:181-190.

Nicholls, J.L. and G.A. Baldassarre. 1990. Habitat associations of piping plovers wintering in the United States. Wilson Bulletin 102:581-590.

Nowlin, W.D., Jr. 1972. Winter circulation patterns and property distributions. In: Capurra, L.R.A. and J.L. Reid, eds. Contributions on the Physical Oceanography of the Gulf of Mexico. Houston, TX: Gulf Publishing Company. Pp. 3-51.

Nowlin, W.D., Jr., A.E. Jochens, R.O. Reid, and S.F. DiMarco. 1998. Texas-Louisiana shelf circulation and transport processes study: Synthesis report. Volume II: Appendices. U.S. Dept. of the Interior, Minerals Management Services, Gulf of Mexico OCS Region, New Orleans, LA. OCS Study MMS 98-0036. 288 pp.

Olds, W.T., Jr. 1984. In: U.S. Congress, House, Committee on Merchant Marine Fisheries, Offshore Oil and Gas Activity and Its Socioeconomic and Environmental Influences, 98th Cong., 2d sess., 1984. Pp. 54-55.

Owens, D. 1983. Oil and sea turtles in the Gulf of Mexico: A proposal to study the problem. U.S. Dept. of the Interior, Fish and Wildlife Service, Biological Services Program. WS/OBS-83/03. Pp. 34-39.

Parnell, J.F., D.G. Ainley, H. Blokpoel, B. Cain, T.W. Custer, J.L. Dusi, S. Kress, J.A. Kushlan, W.E. Southern, L.E. Stenzel, and B.C. Thompson. 1988. Colonial waterbird management in North America. Colonial Waterbirds 11:129-345.

Paruka, F. 2007. Personal communication. Information concerning the critical habitat, sampling programs, and damage assessments of the Gulf Sturgeon. U.S. Dept. of the Interior, Fish and Wildlife Service, Ecological Services, Fisheries Resource Office, Panama City, FL. May 29, 2007.

Patrick, L. 1997. Personal communication. U.S. Dept. of the Interior, Fish and Wildlife Service, Panama City, FL.

Payne, J.F., J. Kiceniuk, L.L. Fancey, U. Williams, G.L. Fletcher, A. Rahimtula, and B. Fowler. 1988. What is a safe level of polycyclic aromatic hydrocarbons for fish: Subchronic toxicity study on winter flounder (*Pseudopleuronectes americanus*). Can. J. Fish. Aquat. Sci. 45:1983-1993.

Pearson, C.E., and S.R. James, Jr., M.C. Krivor, and S.D. El Darragi. 2003. Refining and revising the Gulf of Mexico Outer Continental Shelf region high-probability model for historic shipwrecks. 3 vols. U.S. Dept. of the Interior, Minerals Management Service, Gulf of Mexico OCS Region, New Orleans, LA. OCS Study MMS 2003-060, 2003-061, and 2003-062. 13, 338, and 138 pp., respectively.

Pequegnat, W.E. 1983. The ecological communities of the continental slope and adjacent regimes of the northern Gulf of Mexico. Prepared by TerEco Corp. for the U.S. Dept. of the Interior, Minerals Management Service, New Orleans, LA. Contract no. AA851-CT1-12. 398 pp.

Raymond, P.W. 1984. Sea turtle hatchling disorientation and artificial beachfront lighting: A review of the problem and potential solutions. Washington, DC: Center for Environmental Education. 72 pp.

Reggio, V.C., Jr. 1987. Rigs-to-Reefs: The use of obsolete petroleum structures as artificial reefs. U.S. Dept. of the Interior, Minerals Management Service, Gulf of Mexico OCS Region, New Orleans, LA. OCS Report MMS 87-0015. 17 pp.

Renger, E. and K. Bednarczyk. 1986. Sediment transport by ship traffic in offshore channels. Kueste 44:89-132.

Richardson, W.J., C.R. Greene, C.I. Mame, and D.H. Thomson. 1995. Marine mammals and noise. San Diego, CA: Academic Press Inc.

Ronconi, R.A., C.C. St. Clair, P.D. O'Hara, and A.E. Burger. 2004. Waterbird deterrence at oil spills and other hazardous sites: potential applications of a radar-activated on-demand deterrence system. Marine Ornithology 32:25-33.

Rowe, G.T. and M.C. Kennicutt II. 2002. Deepwater program: Northern Gulf of Mexico continental slope habitat and benthic ecology. Year 2: Interim report. U.S. Dept. of the Interior, Minerals Management Service, Gulf of Mexico OCS Region, New Orleans, LA. OCS Study MMS 2002-063. 158 pp.

Rowley K. 2007. GulfGov reports: A year and a half after Katrina and Rita, an uneven recovery. Nelson A. Rockefeller Institute of Government, Albany, NY, and Public Affairs Research Council of Louisiana, Baton Rouge, LA. 73 pp. Internet website: http://www.rockinst.org/WorkArea/showcontent.aspx?id=9920.

Russell, M., J. Holcomb, and A. Berkner. 2003. 30-years of oiled wildlife response statistics. In: Proceedings of the 7th International Conference on the Effects of Oil on Wildlife, Hamburg, Germany, 14-16 October, 2003.

Sassen, R., J.M. Brooks, M.C. Kennicutt II, I.R. MacDonald, and N.L. Guinasso, Jr. 1993a. How oil seeps, discoveries relate in deepwater Gulf of Mexico. Oil and Gas Journal 91(16):64-69.

Sassen, R., H.H. Roberts, P. Aharon, J. Larkin, E.W. Chinn, and R. Carney. 1993b. Chemosynthetic bacterial mats at cold hydrocarbon seeps, Gulf of Mexico continental slope. Organic Geochemistry 20(1):77-89.

Slack, T. 2007. Personal communication. Information concerning the State of Mississippi Gulf sturgeon sampling and tagging program. Mississippi State Museum of Natural History. June 4, 2007.

Spalding, E.A. and M.W. Hester. 2007. Effects of hydrology and salinity on oligohaline plant species productivity: Implications of relative sea-level rise. Journal of Estuaries and Coasts. View abstract at http://www.erf.org/cesn/vol30n2r4.html.

Spies, R.B., J.S. Felton, and L. Dillard. 1982. Hepatic mixed-function oxidases in California flatfishes are increased in contaminated environments and by oil and PCB ingestion. Mar. Biol. 70:117-127.

Terrell, D. and R. Bilbo. 2007. A report on the impact of Hurricanes Katrina and Rita on Louisiana businesses: 2005Q2-2006Q2. Louisiana State University, Division of Economic Development, Baton Rouge, LA. 41 pp. Internet website: http://www.bus.lsu.edu/centers/ded/. Accessed March 2007.

Terres, J.K. 1991. The Audubon Society encyclopedia of North American birds. New York: Wing Books. 1,109 pp.

Thompson, N.B. 1988. The status of loggerhead, *Caretta caretta*; Kemp's ridley, *Lepidochelys kempi*; and green, *Chelonia mydas*, sea turtles in U.S. waters. Marine Fisheries Review 50(3):16-23.

Tolbert, C.M. and M. Sizer. 1996. U.S. commuting zones and labor market areas: 1990 update. U.S. Dept. of Agriculture, Economic Research Service, Rural Economy Division. Staff Paper No. AGES-9614.

U.S. Dept. of Commerce. National Oceanic and Atmospheric Administration. 1992. Oil spill case histories 1967-1991: Summaries of significant U.S. and international spills. U.S. Dept. of Commerce, National Oceanic and Atmospheric Administration, Hazardous Materials Response and Assessment Division, Report No. HMRAD-92-11, Seattle, WA. September 1992. http://response.restoration.noaa.gov/oilaids/spilldb.pdf

U.S. Dept. of Commerce. National Oceanic and Atmospheric Administration. National Hurricane Center. 2006. U.S. mainland hurricane strikes by state, 1851-2004. Internet website: http://www.nhc.noaa.gov/paststate.shtml. Accessed October 24, 2006.

U.S. Dept. of Commerce. National Oceanic and Atmospheric Administration/National Marine Fisheries Service. 2007. Impact of Hurricanes Katrina, Rita, and Wilma on commercial and recreational fishery habitat of Alabama, Florida, Louisiana, Mississippi, and Texas. Internet website: http://www.nmfs.noaa.gov/msa2007/docs/HurricaneImpactsHabitat_080707_1200.pdf. Accessed September 2007.

U.S. Dept. of Commerce. National Marine Fisheries Service. 2007. Information and databases on fisheries landings. Internet website (latest data for 2006): http://www.st.nmfs.gov/st1/commercial/landings/annual_landings.html.

U.S. Dept. of Labor. Bureau of Labor Statistics. 2006. Review: Special issue – Hurricane Katrina. Monthly Labor Review 129(8):78 pp. August 2006. Internet website: http://www.stats.bls.gov/opub/mlr/2006/08/contents.htm. Accessed June 1, 2007.

U.S. Dept. of Labor. Bureau of Labor Statistics. 2007. News – Regional and state employment and unemployment: April 2007. U.S. Dept. of Labor, Bureau of Labor Statistics, Washington, DC. USDL 07-0713. Internet website: http://www.bls.gov/news.release/archives/laus_09252007.pdf.

U.S. Dept. of the Interior. Fish and Wildlife Service. 1994. Whooping crane recovery plan (second revision) Southeastern states bald eagle recover plan. U.S. Dept. of the Interior, Fish and Wildlife Service, Albuquerque, NM. 92 pp.

U.S. Dept. of the Interior. Fish and Wildlife Service. 2001. Endangered and threatened wildlife and plants; final determinations of critical habitat for wintering piping plovers; final rule. *Federal Register*, 66 FR 132, pp 36037-36086.

U.S. Dept. of the Interior. Fish and Wildlife Service. 2007a. Gulf sturgeon recovery. Internet website: http://www.fws.gov/panamacity/programs/gulfsturg-recov.html. Accessed May 29, 2007.

U.S. Dept. of the Interior. Fish and Wildlife Service. 2007b. Critical habitat of the Gulf sturgeon. Internet website: http://www.fws.gov/alabama/gs. Accessed May 29, 2007.

U.S. Dept. of the Interior. Fish and Wildlife Service. 2007c. Endangered and threatened wildlife and plants; removing the bald eagle in the lower 48 States from the list of endangered and threatened wildlife, final rule; draft post-delisting and monitoring plan for the bald eagle (*Haliaeetus leucocephalus*) and proposed information collection; notice. 50 CFR 17. *Federal Register*, 72 FR 130, pp. 37346-37371. July 9, 2007, Rules and Regulations.

U.S. Dept. of the Interior. Geological Survey. 2005. Post Hurricane Katrina flights over Louisiana's barrier islands. Internet website: http://www.nwrc.usgs.gov/hurricane/katrina-post-hurricane-flights.htm. Accessed September 2007.

U.S. Dept. of the Interior. Minerals Management Service. 1997. Gulf of Mexico OCS oil and gas lease Sales 169, 172, 175, 178 and 182: Central Planning Area, final environmental impact statement. U.S. Dept. of the Interior, Minerals Management Service, Gulf of Mexico OCS Region, New Orleans, LA. OCS EIS/EA MMS 97-0033.

U.S. Dept. of the Interior. Minerals Management Service. 2000a. Gulf of Mexico deepwater operations and activities: Environmental assessment. U.S. Dept. of the Interior, Minerals Management Service, Gulf of Mexico OCS Region, New Orleans, LA. OCS EIS/EA MS 2000-001. 264 pp.

U.S. Dept. of the Interior. Minerals Management Service. 2000b. Marine riser failure: Safety Alert No. 186. U.S. Dept. of the Interior, Minerals Management Service, Gulf of Mexico OCS Region, New Orleans, LA. March 3, 2000.

U.S. Dept. of the Interior. Minerals Management Service. 2001. Gulf of Mexico OCS oil and gas lease Sale 181, Eastern Planning Area—final environmental impact statement. U.S. Dept. of the Interior, Minerals Management Service, Gulf of Mexico OCS Region, New Orleans, LA. OCS EIS/EA MMS 2001-051. 2 vols.

U.S. Dept. of the Interior. Minerals Management Service. 2002. Programmatic environmental assessment for Grid 16: Site-specific evaluation of BP Exploration and Production, Inc.'s initial development operations coordination document, N-7459; Thunder Horse Project, Mississippi Canyon Block 777 Unit (Blocks 775, 776, 777, 778, 819, 820, 821, and 822). U.S. Dept. of the Interior, Minerals Management Service, Gulf of Mexico OCS Region, New Orleans, LA. OCS EIS/EA MMS 2002-081. 165 pp.

U.S. Dept. of the Interior. Minerals Management Service. 2003a. Programmatic environmental assessment for Grid 13: Site-specific evaluation of Anadarko Petroleum Corporation's initial development operations coordination document, N-7753; Marco Polo Project, Green Canyon Block 608. U.S. Dept. of the Interior, Minerals Management Service, Gulf of Mexico OCS Region, New Orleans, LA. OCS EIS/EA MMS 2003-067. 115 pp.

U.S. Dept. of the Interior. Minerals Management Service. 2003b. Marine riser failure. Safety Alert No. 213. U.S. Dept. of the Interior, Minerals Management Service, Gulf of Mexico OCS Region, New Orleans, LA. June 11, 2003.

U.S. Dept. of the Interior. Minerals Management Service. 2003c. Marine riser failure. Safety Alert No. 213. U.S. Dept. of the Interior, Minerals Management Service, Gulf of Mexico OCS Region, New Orleans, LA. June 11, 2003.

U.S. Dept. of the Interior. Minerals Management Service. 2007. Gulf of Mexico OCS oil and gas lease Sales: 2007-2012 Western Planning Area Sales 204, 207, 210, 215, and 218; Central Planning Area Sales 205, 206, 208, 213, 216, and 222—final environmental impact statement Volume I. U.S. Dept. of the Interior, Minerals Management Service, Gulf of Mexico OCS Region, New Orleans, LA. OCS EIS/EA MMS 2007-018.

U.S. Dept. of the Interior. Minerals Management Service. 2008. Gulf of Mexico OCS oil and gas lease sales: 2009-2012; Central Planning Area Sales 208, 213, 216, and 222; Western Planning Area Sales 210, 215, and 218—draft supplemental environmental impact statement. U.S. Dept. of the Interior, Minerals Management Service, Gulf of Mexico OCS Region, New Orleans, LA. OCS EIS/EA MMS 2008-011.

U.S. Dept. of Transportation. Federal Aviation Administration. 2004. Visual flight rules near noise-sensitive areas. Advisory Circular No. 91-36D; September 17, 2004.

U.S. Environmental Protection Agency. 2004. National coastal condition report II. U.S. Environmental Protection Agency, Office of Research and Development, Office of Water, Washington DC. EPA-620/R-03/002.

Velando, A., D. Alvarez, J. Mourino, F. Arcos, and A. Barros. 2005. Population trends and reproductive success of the European shag *Phalacrocorax aristotelis* on the Iberian Peninsula following the *Prestige* oil spill. Journal of Ornithology 146:116-120.

Webb, J.W., G.T. Tanner, and B.H. Koerth. 1981. Oil spill effects on smooth cordgrass in Galveston Bay, Texas. Contributions in Marine Science 24:107-114.

Webb, J.W., S.K. Alexander, and J.K. Winters. 1985. Effects of autumn application of oil on *Spartina alterniflora* in a Texas salt marsh. Environ. Poll., Series A 38(4):321-337.

Webb, J.W. 1988. Establishment of vegetation on oil-contaminated dunes. *Shore and Beach*, October. Pp. 20-23.

Williams, J.H. and I.W. Duedall. 1997. Florida hurricanes and tropical storms; revised edition. Gainesville, FL: The University of Florida Press. 146 pp.

Witherington, B.E. 1997. The problem of photopollution for sea turtles and other nocturnal animals. In: Clemmons, J.R. and R. Buchholz, eds. Behavioral approaches to conservation in the wild. Cambridge, England: Cambridge University Press. Pp. 303-328.

Witherington, B.E. and R.E. Martin. 1996. Understanding, assessing, and resolving light-pollution problems on sea turtle nesting beaches. Florida Marine Research Institute Technical Report TR-2, Florida Dept. of Environmental Protection. 73 pp.

Woods & Poole Economics, Inc. 2006. The 2006 Complete Economic and Demographic Data Source (CEDDS) on CD-ROM.

Woods and Poole Economics, Inc. 2007. The 2007 Complete Economic and Demographic Data Source (CEEDS) on CD-ROM.

6. PREPARERS

NEPA Coordinator

Alvin Jones	Physical Scientist

Contributors

Pat Adkins	Information Management Specialist
David Ball	Archaeologist—Archaeological Issues
Greg Boland	Biologist—Fisheries and Benthic Issues
Darice Breeding	Physical Scientist—Hydrocarbon Spill Issues
Donald Glenn	Biologist—Marine Mammals and Sea Turtles Issues
Mike Gravois	GIS/Visual Information Specialist
Larry Hartzog	Biologist—Barrier Beaches and Dune Issues
Bonnie Johnson	Environmental Scientist—Coastal Zone Management Issues
Jill Leale	GIS/Visual Information Specialist
Harry Luton	Sociologist—Recreation and Environmental Justice Issues
Stacie Meritt-Hendon	Physical Scientist—Air Quality Issues
Margaret Metcalf	Physical Scientist—Water Quality Issues
Deborah Miller	Technical Publications Editor
Dave Moran	Environmental Scientist—Marine and Coastal Birds Issues
Maureen Mulino	Marine Biologist—Commercial Fisheries Issues
Cathy Rosa	Environmental Assessment Program Specialist
Kristen Strellec	Economist—Socioeconomic Issues

Reviewers and Supervisors

Gary Goeke	Supervisor, NEPA/CZM Coordination Unit
Dennis Chew	Chief, Environmental Assessment Section

7. APPENDICES

Appendix A

Waste and Discharges Review

APPENDIX A.   WASTE AND DISCHARGES REVIEW

The discharge of wastes into offshore waters is regulated by USEPA under the authority of the Clean Water Act. No wastes generated during oil and gas operations can be discharged overboard unless they meet the standards required within an NPDES permit. All of the waste types generated from the proposed exploration activities for Phoenix will be either (1) discharged overboard in compliance with NPDES requirements or (2) transported to shore for disposal in permitted or licensed commercial facilities or for recycling. The wastes for overboard discharge and transport to shore for recycling or disposal are summarized in **Tables A-1 and A-2**, respectively.

Wastes generated during the development and production activities of the Phoenix Project consist of (1) drill fluids; (2) drill cuttings (WBF); (3) sanitary and domestic wastes; (4) deck drainage; (5) well treatment, workover, or completion fluids; (6) excess cement; (7) produced water; (8) used oil; and (9) solid trash and debris. The projected amounts are listed in **Tables A-1 and A-2**. Additional project discharges may include (10) uncontaminated seawater used for cooling, desalinization, and ballast; (11) bilge water, and (12) chemically treated seawater or freshwater.

Well treatment, completion, and workover fluids would be collected in a separator. Aqueous fluids would be routed to the water treatment system for discharge. Nonaqueous fluids would be collected in drums or the slop tank of a supply vessel to be transported to shore for disposal.

Routine sanitary and domestic wastes necessarily arise from people working offshore on drilling rigs, production platforms, and support vessels.

Deck drainage effluent is primarily rainwater containing residual oil and grease from equipment washwater and rainwater. Overboard discharge of deck drainage is governed by the NPDES permit requirement for no visible oil sheen. A maximum for deck drainage during daily operation is estimated by MMS to be 3,000 bbl per month.

Table A-1

Projected Ocean Discharges from the Phoenix Project

Type of Waste	Total Amount Discharged	Discharge Rate	Discharge Method
Water-based mud	2,500 bbl/well	220 bbl/hr	Overboard
Drill cuttings associated with water-based drilling fluids	2,000-3,000 bbl/well		Overboard
Muds and cuttings at the seafloor	Gel–5,000 bbl WBM–8,000 bbl Cuttings–20,000 bbl Seawater and caustic–4,800 bbl Cement–100 bbl		Overboard
Sanitary waste	864,000 gallons	20 gal/person/day	Chlorinate and discharge
Domestic waste	1,296,000 gallons	30 gal/person/day	Remove floating solids and discharge
Deck drainage	0-365 bbl/day	1 bbl/day (dependent on rainfall)	Treat for oil and grease and discharge
Well treatment, workover, or completion fluids	1,300 bbl/well		Discharge used fluids overboard, return excess to shore for credit
Produced water	250,000 bbl/year	1,000 bbl/day	

Table A-2

Wastes for Transport to Shore on the Proposed Phoenix Project

Type of Waste—Approximate Composition	Amount	Name/Location of Disposal Facility	Treatment and/or Storage, Transport, and Disposal Method
Trash and debris	216 ft³	Riverside Recycle	Transport to shore base for recycle and burn
Hazardous liquid—used oil	10 bbl	Riverside Recycle	Transport to shore base for recycle

Appendix B

Accidental Oil-Spill Review

ANALYSIS OF THE POTENTIAL FOR AN ACCIDENTAL OIL SPILL AND THE POTENTIAL FOR IMPACTS FROM THE PHOENIX DEVELOPMENT PROJECT – GRID 9, GREEN CANYON BLOCKS 236 AND 237

Introduction

The National Environmental Policy Act requires Federal agencies to consider potential environmental impacts (direct, indirect, and cumulative) of proposed actions as part of agency planning and decisionmaking. The NEPA analyses address many issues relating to potential impacts, including issues that may have a very low probability of occurrence, but which the public considers important or for which the environmental consequences could be significant.

The past several decades of spill data show that accidental oil spills ($\geq$1,000 bbl) associated with oil and gas exploration and development are low-probability events in Federal OCS waters of the GOM, yet the issue of oil spills is important to the public. This appendix summarizes key information about the probability of accidental spills from offshore oil and gas activities in the GOM.

Spill Prevention

The MMS has comprehensive pollution-prevention requirements that include numerous redundant levels of safety devices, as well as inspection and testing requirements to confirm that these devices work. Many of these requirements have been in place since about 1980. Spill trends analysis for the GOM OCS shows that spills from facilities have decreased over time, indicating that MMS's engineering and safety requirements have minimized the potential for spill occurrence and associated impacts. Details regarding MMS's engineering and safety requirements can be found at 30 CFR 250.800 Subpart H.

OCS Spills in the Past

This summary of past OCS spills presents data for the period 1985-1999. The 1985-1999 time period was chosen to reflect more modern engineering and regulatory requirements and because OCS spill rates are available for this period. For the period 1985-1999, there were no spills $\geq$1,000 bbl from OCS platforms, eight spills $\geq$1,000 bbl from OCS pipelines, and no spills $\geq$1,000 bbl from OCS blowouts (**Tables B-1 through B-3**). The Multisale EIS and EPA Sale 224 Supplemental EIS (USDOI, MMS, 2007a and b, respectively) provide additional information on past OCS spills.

Estimating Future Potential Spills

The MMS estimates the risk of future potential spills by multiplying variables to result in a numerical expression of risk. These variables include the potential of a spill occurring based on historical OCS spill rates and a variable for the potential for a spill to be transported to environmental resources based on trajectory modeling. The following subsections describe the spill occurrence and transport variables used to estimate risk and the risk calculation for the proposed action.

Spill Occurrence Variable (SOV) Representing the Potential for a Spill

The SOV is derived based on past OCS spill frequency. That is, data from past OCS spills are used to estimate future potential OCS spills. The MMS has estimated spill rates for spills from the following sources: facilities, pipelines, and drilling.

Spill rates for facilities and pipelines have been developed for several time periods and an analysis of trends for spills is presented in *Update of Comparative Occurrence Rates for Offshore Oil Spills* (Anderson and LaBelle, 2000). Spill rates for the most recent period analyzed, 1985-1999, are presented here. Data for this recent period should reflect more modern spill-prevention requirements. A review of recent historical data following Hurricane Katrina indicates that there has been no change in the rates identified in the aforementioned study/assessment.

Spill rates for facilities and pipelines are based on the number of spills per volume of oil handled. Spill rates for blowouts are based on the number of blowouts with a release of oil per number of wells drilled. Spill rates for the period 1985-1999 are shown in **Table B-4**. It should be noted that there were no platform or blowout spills ≥1,000 bbl for the period 1985-1999. Use of "zero" spills would result in a zero spill rate. To allow for conservative future predictions of spill occurrence, a spill number of one was "assigned" to provide a non-zero spill rate for blowouts. The spill period was expanded to 1980 to include a spill for facilities. While there were no facility or blowout spills during the 1985-1999 period for which data are available, spills could occur in the future. In fact, a pipeline spill ≥1,000 bbl was reported subsequent to this period, so it is reasonable to include a spill to provide a non-zero spill rate. Spill rates are combined with site-specific data on production or pipeline volumes or number of wells being drilled to result in a site-specific SOV.

Transport Variable (TV) Representing the Potential for a Spill to be Transported to Important Environmental Resources

The TV is derived using a trajectory model. This model predicts the direction that winds and currents would transport spills. The model uses an extensive database of observed and theoretically computed ocean currents and fields that represent a statistical estimate of winds and currents that would occur over the life of an oil and gas project, which may span several decades. This model produces the TV that can be combined with other variables, such as the SOV, to estimate the risk of future potential spills and impacts.

Risk Calculation for the Proposed Action

Energy Resource Technology, Inc. proposes to drill and complete two new wells in Green Canyon Block 236, drill and complete four new wells in Green Canyon Block 237, install a subsea manifold, clear the area of debris, and produce from a floating production unit. **Table B-5** presents an estimate of spill risk from the facility and to resources. The risk estimate for the facility was calculated using the spill rate of 0.13 per billion barrels of oil produced, the estimated production for the proposed action, and oil-spill trajectory calculations.

The coastline and associated environmental resources are presented in **Table B-5**. The final column in **Table B-5** presents the result of combining the SOV's and the TV's. The risk of a coastal spill impact from the facility could be considered to be so low as to be near zero.

The Multisale EIS and EPA Sale 224 Supplemental EIS (USDOI, MMS, 2007a and b, respectively) provide additional information on spills and potential impacts. The following section provides additional information regarding MMS's spill-response preparedness requirements.

Spill Response

The MMS has extensive requirements for preparedness to respond to a spill in the event of an accidental spill. This section presents information on MMS requirements for spill-response preparedness.

MMS Spill-Response Program

The MMS Oil-Spill Program oversees the review of oil-spill response plans, coordinates inspection of oil-spill response equipment, and conducts unannounced oil-spill drills. This program also supports continuing research to foster improvements in spill prevention and response. Studies funded by MMS address issues such as spill prevention and response, *in-situ* burning, and dispersant use.

In addition, MMS works with USCG and other members of the multiagency National Response System to further improve spill-response capability in the GOM. The combined resources of these groups and the resources of commercially contracted oil-spill response organizations result in extensive equipment and trained personnel for spill response in the GOM.

Spill Response for this Project

The subject operator has an oil-spill response plan on file with MMS and has a current contract with the offshore oil-spill response organization Clean Gulf Associates.

Potential spill sources during the life of this development project (5 years) would include an accidental blowout (worst case estimated to be approximately 21,000 bbl/day), a spill of liquid oil stored on the platform (approximately 1,850 bbl total storage capacity including flowlines on the facility), a spill of liquid oil stored on the semi-submersible rig (approximately 19,000 total storage capacity), a spill of liquid oil stored on the associated vessels (capacity of the largest vessel is 2,000 bbl), or a spill from the associated oil flowlines or the export pipelines. The operator has demonstrated spill-response preparedness for accidental releases in their oil-spill response plan. Details regarding a proposed response to this facility are included in the proposed plan.

The MMS will continue to verify the operator's capability to respond to oil spills via the MMS Oil-Spill Program. The operator is required to keep their oil-spill response plan up-to-date in accordance with MMS regulations. The operator must also conduct an annual drill to demonstrate the adequacy of their spill preparedness.

Table B-1

Historical Record of OCS Spills ≥1,000 Barrels from OCS Facilities, 1985-1999

Spill Date	Area and Block (water depth and distance from shore)	Volume Spilled (barrels)	Cause of Spill

No OCS facility spills ≥1,000 bbl during the period 1985-1999.

Table B-2

Historical Record of OCS Spills ≥1,000 Barrels from OCS Pipelines, 1985-1999

Spill Date	Area and Block (water depth and distance from shore)	Volume Spilled (barrels)	Cause of Spill
February 7, 1988	South Pass 60 (75 ft, 3.4 mi)	15,576	Service vessel's anchor damaged pipeline
January 24, 1990	Ship Shoal 281 (197 ft, 60 mi)	14,423*	Anchor drag, flange and valve broke off
May 6, 1990	Eugene Island 314 (230 ft, 78 mi)	4,569	Trawl drag pulled off valve
August 31, 1992	South Pelto 8 (30 ft, 6 mi)	2,000	Hurricane Andrew, loose drilling rig's anchor drag damaged pipeline
November 22, 1994	Ship Shoal 281 (197 ft, 60 mi)	4,533*	Trawl drag
January 26, 1998	East Cameron 334 (264 ft, 105 mi)	1,211*	Service vessel's anchor drag damaged pipeline during rescue operation
September 29, 1988	South Pass 38 (110 ft, 6 mi)	8,212	Hurricane Georges, mudslide parted pipeline
July 23, 1999	Ship Shoal 241 (133 ft, 50 mi)	3,189	Jack-up barge sat on pipeline

*condensate

Table B-3

Historical Record of OCS Spills ≥1,000 Barrels from OCS Blowouts, 1985-1999

Spill Date	Area and Block (water depth and distance from shore)	Volume Spilled (barrels)	Cause of Spill

No OCS blowout spills ≥1,000 bbl during the period 1985-1999.

Table B-4

Spill Rates Used to Estimate the Future Potential for Spills

Spill Source	Volume of Oil Handled in Billions of Barrels	Number of Wells Drilled	No. of Spills ≥1,000 Barrels	Risk of Spill from Facilities or Pipelines per Billion Barrels	Risk of Spill from Drilling Blowout per Well
Facilities	7.41 [a]	Not Applicable	1 [a]	>0 to <0.13	Not Applicable
Pipelines	5.81	Not Applicable	8	1.38	Not Applicable
Drilling	Not Applicable	14,067	1 [b]	Not Applicable	>0 to <0.00007

[a] There were actually zero spills ≥1,000 bbl from facilities during the period 1985-1999. The data shown represent 1980-1999. The spill period for facility spills was expanded to 1980 to include a spill for facilities to result in a nonzero risk.

[b] There have been no spills ≥1,000 bbl from blowouts during the period 1985-1999. One spill was "assigned" to provide a non-zero spill rate.

[c] There were no facility or blowout spills ≥1,000 bbl for the period 1985-1999; however, a non-zero spill rate was calculated by expanding the facility period to 1980 and by "assigning" a blowout spill. Therefore, the spill rates for these categories are presented as >0 but below the rates calculated by expanding the data period and assigning a spill.

Table B-5

Spill Risk Estimate for Facilities[1]

Environmental Resource (county/parish)	Spill Occurrence Variable[2] (%)	Transport Variable for Spill Launch Area (LA) 43[3] within 3/10/30 Days (%)	Spill Risk[1,4] within 3/10/30 Days for LA 43 (%)
Matagorda, Tex.	0.47	<0.5/<0.5/2	<0.5/<0.5/<0.5
Brazoria, Tex.	0.47	<0.5/<0.5/1	<0.5/<0.5/<0.5
Galveston, Tex.	0.47	<0.5/<0.5/3	<0.5/<0.5/<0.5
Jefferson, Tex.	0.47	<0.5/<0.5/2	<0.5/<0.5/<0.5
Cameron, La.	0.47	<0.5/1/7	<0.5/<0.5/<0.5
Vermilion, La.	0.47	<0.5/<0.5/3	<0.5/<0.5/<0.5
Iberia, La.	0.47	<0.5/<0.5/1	<0.5/<0.5/<0.5
St Mary, La.	0.47	<0.5/<0.5/<0.5	<0.5/<0.5/<0.5
Terrebonne, La.	0.47	<0.5/<0.5/3	<0.5/<0.5/<0.5
Lafourche, La.	0.47	<0.5/<0.5/1	<0.5/<0.5/<0.5
Jefferson, La.	0.47	<0.5/<0.5/<0.5	<0.5/<0.5/<0.5
Plaquemines, La.	0.47	<0.5/<0.5/2	<0.5/<0.5/<0.5

[1] This combined risk analysis covers only the FPU and subsea wells since the right-of-way pipeline application associated with the project has not yet been submitted and is likely to cover additional spill launch areas. A determination of these spill launch areas is not practical at this time since the exact route of the projected right-of-way pipeline has not been officially proposed by the operator; only tentative plans for the pipeline have been disclosed. However, since a spill from a pipeline transporting the production of the FPU would result in a spill occurrence variable of only 0.5%, the combined risk of occurrence and contact from a leak from the ROW pipeline at the FPU site would also be <0.5%.

[2] The percent chance of a spill event occurring from the proposed Phoenix activities.

[3] The percent chance that winds and currents will move a point projected onto the surface of the Gulf beginning within the area of the proposed project and ending at specified shoreline segments or environmental resources within 30 days. These are the results of a numerical model that calculates the trajectory of a drifting point projected onto the surface of the water using temporally and spatially varying winds and ocean current fields. These probabilities do not factor in the risk of spill occurrence, consideration of the spill size, any spill response or cleanup actions, or any dispersion and weathering of the slick with time. Model results used are for spill launch areas C43 (i.e., CPA, site number).

[4] The probability of a spill occurring and contacting identified environmental features represents the weighted risk that accounts for both the risk that a large spill will occur and the risk that it will contact locations where the resources occur, given the assumptions already described in (1) and (2).

References

Anderson, C.M. and R.P. LaBelle. eds. 2000. Update of comparative occurrence rates for offshore oil spills. Spill Science & Technology Bulletin. 6(5-6):303-321, October-December 2000.

U.S. Dept. of the Interior. Minerals Management Service. 2007a. Gulf of Mexico OCS oil and gas lease sales: 2007-2012; Western Planning Area Sales 204, 207, 210, 215, and 218; Central Planning Area Sales 205, 206, 208, 213, 216, and 222—final environmental impact statement. 2 volumes. U.S. Dept. of the Interior, Minerals Management Service, Gulf of Mexico OCS Region, New Orleans, LA. OCS EIS/EA MMS 2007-018.

U.S. Dept. of the Interior. Minerals Management Service. 2007b. Gulf of Mexico OCS oil and gas
Lease Sale 224: Eastern Planning Area—final supplemental environmental impact statement. U.S.
Dept. of the Interior, Minerals Management Service, Gulf of Mexico OCS Region, New Orleans, LA.
OCS EIS/EA MMS 2007-060.

The Department of the Interior Mission

As the Nation's principal conservation agency, the Department of the Interior has responsibility for most of our nationally owned public lands and natural resources. This includes fostering sound use of our land and water resources; protecting our fish, wildlife, and biological diversity; preserving the environmental and cultural values of our national parks and historical places; and providing for the enjoyment of life through outdoor recreation. The Department assesses our energy and mineral resources and works to ensure that their development is in the best interests of all our people by encouraging stewardship and citizen participation in their care. The Department also has a major responsibility for American Indian reservation communities and for people who live in island territories under U.S. administration.

The Minerals Management Service Mission

As a bureau of the Department of the Interior, the Minerals Management Service's (MMS) primary responsibilities are to manage the mineral resources located on the Nation's Outer Continental Shelf (OCS), collect revenue from the Federal OCS and onshore Federal and Indian lands, and distribute those revenues.

Moreover, in working to meet its responsibilities, the **Offshore Minerals Management Program** administers the OCS competitive leasing program and oversees the safe and environmentally sound exploration and production of our Nation's offshore natural gas, oil and other mineral resources. The MMS **Minerals Revenue Management** meets its responsibilities by ensuring the efficient, timely and accurate collection and disbursement of revenue from mineral leasing and production due to Indian tribes and allottees, States and the U.S. Treasury.

The MMS strives to fulfill its responsibilities through the general guiding principles of: (1) being responsive to the public's concerns and interests by maintaining a dialogue with all potentially affected parties and (2) carrying out its programs with an emphasis on working to enhance the quality of life for all Americans by lending MMS assistance and expertise to economic development and environmental protection.

www.ingramcontent.com/pod-product-compliance
Lightning Source LLC
Chambersburg PA
CBHW080317290526
45790CB00005B/2072